Unholy Trinity
Labor, capital, and land in the new economy

Many of the central results of Classical and Marxian political economy are examples of the self-organization of the capitalist economy as a complex, adaptive system far from equilibrium.

Unholy Trinity explores the relations between contemporary complex systems theory and Classical political economy, and applies the methods it develops to the problems of induced technical change and income distribution in capitalist economies, the control of environmental externalities such as global warming, and the stabilization of world population.

The arguments and methods of this important book address central problems both of economic science and economic policy, and provide fresh paths for theoretical exploration.

Duncan K. Foley is Leo Model Professor of Economics at the Graduate Faculty of New School University, New York City.

The Graz Schumpeter Lectures

Unholy Trinity

Labor, capital, and land
in the new economy

Duncan K. Foley

Routledge
Taylor & Francis Group

LONDON AND NEW YORK

First published 2003
by Routledge
2 Park Square, Milton Park, Abingdon, Oxon, OX14 4RN

Simultaneously published in the USA and Canada
by Routledge
270 Madison Ave, New York NY 10016

Routledge is an imprint of the Taylor & Francis Group

Transferred to Digital Printing 2009

© 2003 Duncan K. Foley

Typeset in Times New Roman by
Newgen Imaging Systems (P) Ltd, Chennai, India

British Library Cataloguing in Publication Data
A catalogue record for this book is available from the British Library

Library of Congress Cataloging in Publication Data
A catalog record for this book has been requested

ISBN10: 0-415-31079-2 (hbk)
ISBN10: 0-415-78020-9 (pbk)

ISBN13: 978-0-415-31079-6 (hbk)
ISBN13: 978-0-415-78020-9 (pbk)

Publisher's Note
The publisher has gone to great lengths to ensure the quality of this reprint
but points out that some imperfections in the original may be apparent.

For Helene and Nico

Contents

4 The new economy and the population of the Earth   75

5 Concluding observations   89

Foreword

The Graz Schumpeter Lectures

On 30 October 1911 Joseph Schumpeter (1883–1950) was appointed by Emperor Francis Joseph Professor of Political Economy in the University of Graz, in Schumpeter's words "the most agreeable university in Austria." He remained a faculty member until 1922. Schumpeter used to call the thirties in a scholar's life "the scared decade of fertility." True to his belief, the publication of the German original of the *Theory of Economic Development* coincided with Schumpeter's arrival in Graz. A string of well-known works such as *Economic Doctrine and Method, The Crisis of the Tax State* and *Zur Soziologie der Imperialismen* bear testimony to the extraordinary productivity of the period spent in Graz.

The Graz Schumpeter Society was founded in 1995. Generous financial support from the Government of Styria promoted the inauguration of the Graz Schumpeter Lectures in the same year. Meanwhile, the Lectures are firmly established in the pertinent intellectual community. A search committee appoints the Graz Schumpeter Lecturer for a particular year. Lecturers are chosen on the merits of their original contribution to scholarship. The Lectures aim at the frontiers of knowledge in areas of research distinguished by rapid innovation and potential applicability of their results in economic and political decision making. While the Lectures are named after Joseph Schumpeter, their concern is by no means confined to his life and work. In Schumpeter's spirit, lecturers are encouraged to transgress conventional disciplinary boundaries and to enquire into more inclusive views of the social world.

Stephan Boehm
Chairman, Graz Schumpeter Society

Acknowledgments

I would like to thank the Schumpeter Society for the invitation to deliver these lectures, and the University of Graz and its Department of Economics for the warm welcome I found in Graz. Heinz Kurz's friendship and support has been invaluable to me in completing this work. Sam Bowles, Gérard Duménil and Dominique Lévy, Tom Michl, Karaswamy Velupillai, and Sergio Parrinello have taken the trouble to give me helpful comments on various aspects of this book. Alexander J. Julius provided me with crucial bibliographic suggestions and a sustained critical dialogue on the issues discussed here. The book has also benefitted from comments and reactions at seminars at the Universities of Rome I and III, the University of Pisa, the University of Frankfurt, and the University of Siena. Much of Chapter 4 has been reprinted from my article, Stabilization of human population through economic increasing returns. *Economic Letters*, 68(3), pp. 309–17, 2000, with permission from Elsevier.

Duncan K. Foley

1 Complexity, self-organization, and political economy

Introduction

My theme in this book is the capacity of the methods of the Classical political economists, Adam Smith, Thomas Malthus, David Ricardo, and their critic, Karl Marx, to reveal the self-organizing character of the capitalist economy regarded as a complex, adaptive, non-equilibrium system.

From one point of view this is an exercise in anachronism, since the language of complex systems theory and its application to economic problems is only about forty years old, and it is implausible to claim that Smith or Ricardo or Marx thought about the problems of the economy using the conceptual tools of complexity science. On the other hand, I will argue that the language and vision of the Classical political economists incorporates many insights of contemporary complex systems theory. There are also indirect but important intellectual pathways that connect the Classical political economists of the eighteenth and nineteenth centuries to the twentieth century emergence of complexity science. I also will argue that complexity theory sheds some light on the extraordinary effectiveness of the Classical political economists' methods and the depth of their analytical results. I believe that contemporary economists still have much to learn from these methods and results about the capitalist economy and its evolution.

What is a complex system?

Complexity theory represents an ambitious effort to analyze the functioning of highly organized but decentralized systems composed of very large numbers of individual components. The basic processes of life, involving the chemical interaction of thousands of proteins, the living cell, which localizes and organizes these processes, the human brain in which thousands of cells interact to maintain consciousness, ecological systems arising from the interaction of thousands of species, the process of biological evolution from which new species emerges, and the capitalist economy, which arises from the interaction of millions of human individuals, each of them already a complex entity, are leading examples. Some introductions to the concepts of complex systems theory are Cowan *et al.* (1994), Kauffman (1995), Albin and Foley (1998), Wolfram (2002). A good introduction to the mathematics of complexity theory is Casti (1992, ch. 9).

Complexity theory starts from the bold and controversial conjecture that these diverse systems have important features in common that transcend their apparent differences in scale, material components, and organizing laws of motion. What these systems share are a potential to configure their component parts in an astronomically large number of ways (they are *complex*), constant change in response to environmental stimulus and their own development (they are *adaptive*), a strong tendency to achieve recognizable, stable patterns in their configuration (they are *self-organizing*), and an avoidance of stable, self-reproducing states (they are *non-equilibrium systems*). The task complexity science sets itself is the exploration of the general properties of complex, adaptive, self-organizing, non-equilibrium systems.

The methods of complex systems theory are highly empirical and inductive. The complex systems scientist tends to study the properties of particular simplified and abstract models of complex systems. These models often involve the study of the interaction of large numbers of highly stylized and simplified components in computer simulations, with the aim of identifying generalizable properties of adaptability and self-organization common to a wide range of complex systems. A characteristic of these stylized complex systems is that their components and rules of interaction, though they are often very much simpler than real neurons or proteins or capitalist firms, are *non-linear*, that is, that they exhibit qualitative differences in their behavior in response to stimulus of different intensities and scales. The computer plays a critical role in this research, because it becomes impossible to say much directly about the dynamics of non-linear systems with a large number of degrees of freedom using classical mathematical analytical methods.

There are many potential pitfalls in this research project. Most of these arise from the difficulty of verifying the general character of the specific phenomena observed in particular models. A pattern of self-organization, for example, may turn out to reflect a particular symmetry of interaction implicit in the model system, and thus not to appear in similar systems that lack this symmetry. Skeptics question the premise that complex systems share any general determinable properties. The record of complexity research has not put these doubts to rest. Its triumphs remain largely in the realm of brilliant insights connected to particular models, and a unified synthesis remains an elusive goal. Nonetheless, the methods of complex systems science have had a growing impact on research in a wide range of fields, not least in economics. The vision of explaining complex and adaptive order as emerging from the interaction of large numbers of relatively simple components according to relatively simple laws presents a compelling challenge to many researchers.

The Classical political economic vision

The great theme of the Classical political economists was that individual economic actions have unintended social consequences. Economic life in the large is thus organized and coherent in a way that no single economic actor envisions or controls.

Smith

The most powerful example of this effect is the Classical conception of competition, enunciated, if not originated, in Adam Smith's *Wealth of Nations* (1937). Smith observes that each owner of "stock" (capital) will seek to maximize its potential rate of growth, that is, its profit rate, by investing in the line of production he judges to be most promising. Capital, according to Smith's vision, will be disinvested from lines of production with relatively low profit rates, and moved to lines of production with relatively high profit rates. The intention of wealth-owners in reallocating capital in this way is to maximize their own rate of profit, but the effect of their actions is to *equalize* profit rates tendentially between different lines of production. This equalization of profit rates, which is of no particular interest to individual capitalists, is also the condition for maximizing the profit rate of the aggregate national capital, that is, the wealth of the nation.

Smith and the Classical political economists who followed him did not believe that this competitive process would lead to an actual equalization of realized or prospective profit rates at any moment in time. The movement of capital from one line of production to another would upset the conditions of other lines of production, which, together with disturbances from outside the national economy, would always prevent the realization of a state of equalization of profit rates. They expected to see a ceaseless fluctuation of prices and profit rates as the outcome of the competitive process, rather than the achievement of a state of "equilibrium" in which prices settled down to levels ("natural prices") at which profit rates would be equalized. Nonetheless, the *concept* of this equilibrium state (which has come to be referred to as "long-period" equilibrium) plays a natural and important part in the analysis of the real economy. The competitive dynamic, even if it is not stable in the mathematical sense of pushing the system to an equilibrium of equal profit rates, will prevent prices and profit rates from wandering indefinitely far from their equilibrium values. This idea is expressed by arguing that observed market prices tend to *gravitate* around the natural prices at which profit rates would be equalized. The *abstract* concept of long-period equilibrium natural prices plays a crucial analytical role in understanding the *concrete* fluctuations of observable market prices.

This sophisticated method of reasoning contrasts sharply, and, in my opinion, favorably with the tendency of neoclassical economists to identify observed values of prices with their equilibrium levels in abstract models. The neoclassical vision requires an implausible degree of foresight and coordination of individual plans in its assertion of the attainment of equilibrium as a picture of the operation of the real economy. Furthermore, stable equilibrium systems cannot exhibit complex dynamic behavior, so the neoclassical vision remains blind to the evolutionary, path-dependent, and adaptive character of economic institutions. The Classical vision, on the other hand, is consistent with the complex systems view of the world. It does not insist that each and every component of the economy achieve its own equilibrium as part of a larger master equilibrium of the system as a whole. In fact, it is precisely from the *disequilibrium* behavior of individual households and firms that the Classical vision of competition sees the orderliness of gravitation of market prices around natural prices as arising. In the language of complex systems theory, Classical gravitation is a self-organized outcome of the competitive economic system. From the Classical point of view, competition need not be "perfect" in order to bring about the tendency to self-organization. The self-organization of complex systems is *robust* in the sense that it does not depend on any particular detail of the evolution of the system, and will reassert itself even when some of the mechanisms supporting it are frustrated.

Smith characterizes the capitalist restlessly seeking the highest profit rate on his capital as a "public benefactor" (1937, ch. III), and the coordinated (or, more precisely, self-organized) outcome for the economy as the result of the operation of an "Invisible Hand." But the force of Smith's argument here has often been misunderstood. There is no reason in general why one individual in capitalist society benefits from another individual's increase in wealth. The benefits from individual accumulation lie in the growth of the *national* wealth, which Smith saw as the foundation of its military and diplomatic power. Presumably this effect arises in part because the wealth of individual capitalists is the foundation of the state's taxing power.

But Smith has another, more important, reason for regarding the accumulating capitalist as a public benefactor. Smith argued that the driving force of economic development was the *division of labor* that arises as a result of the widening *extent of the market*. It is precisely the accumulation of capital, in Smith's view, that drives the extent of the market, both by increasing the wealth and income of the population, and increasing population itself. The individual accumulating capitalist enriches himself, which is his intention, but in increasing the market for other capitalists' products, he also indirectly and unintentionally fosters an increase in the division of labor. The ensuing increase in the productivity of labor does benefit the other capitalists and, potentially, workers. The accumulation of capital is thus part of a "virtuous cycle" in Smith's vision. Accumulation increases population, wealth, and income, thus increasing the size of the market, which in its turn fosters a wider and deeper division of labor, increasing labor productivity, profit rates, and accumulation. This self-reinforcing cycle is the basic metabolism of capitalist economic development, responsible both for its creative triumphs and its destructive paroxysms. Smith's endorsement of laissez-faire policies is at its root an affirmation that this process will in the end be good for humanity.

The neoclassical tradition interprets Smith's concepts in quite a different way. Neoclassical analysis identifies the Invisible Hand and laissez-faire policies with the tendency for unfettered competition to achieve an efficient allocation of resources, rather than with the tendency for unfettered capital accumulation to produce a widening division of labor. Smith's notion of a widening division of labor leading to increased labor productivity translates into neoclassical language as *increasing returns* to the application of labor and capital to land. But pervasive increasing returns is incompatible with the establishment of a neoclassical competitive equilibrium except under special analytical assumptions. Thus, the feature of economic life that Smith puts at the center of his vision is a feature that is actually inconsistent with the neoclassical vision of achieving an efficient allocation of resources through competition.

But Smith's vision of the widening and self-reinforcing division of labor is remarkably consistent with the systems theory conception of a complex, self-organizing, non-equilibrium process. Growth and development as irreversible processes are characteristic of complex systems. While particular self-organizing aspects of complex systems may have strong homeostatic properties that lead them to seek recognizable organized states (e.g. like the individual cell in an animal), the systems themselves are open, adaptable, and indeterminate (like the life history of an animal), and not typically subject to simple equilibrium analysis. We know that the wolf, for example, must maintain nutritional balance with her environment to live, but this observation does not allow us to predict her life cycle, where she will migrate, mate, or, eventually, die. Smith's vision of capitalist economic development is analogous: he can explain the metabolic processes, accumulation and competition, that support the evolution of the capitalist economy, but not its history, the specific development of its technology, or its sociology.

Malthus and Ricardo

Smith's great immediate successors were Thomas Malthus and David Ricardo. Their characteristic discoveries were in fact in opposition to Smith's open-ended optimism about the prospects for capitalist economic development, but their methods grow out of Smith's arguments, and reflect the same preoccupation with unintended consequences of human actions.

Malthus (1985) argued that human societies tend to reach a *demographic equilibrium* in which high mortality from disease and malnutrition, especially infant mortality, balanced high fertility. His analysis of this problem centers on a stable feedback mechanism, in the language of modern systems theory. If mortality were to fall below the equilibrium level, the high rate of fertility would increase population. Malthus believed that an increasing population would encounter diminishing returns in the face of limited land and other natural resources, so that the standard of living would fall, increasing the incidence of mortality through malnutrition and disease. Malthus' theory has turned out to be spectacularly inappropriate to understanding the actual process of capitalist development over the succeeding three hundred years. But it is interesting to note that his method of reasoning depends on the same notions of unintended consequences and self-organization as Smith's. Malthus' procreators have no way of knowing that the indirect consequence of their fertility decisions will be a demographic equilibrium. They themselves are not in any kind of "equilibrium" according to Malthus' argument. The limitations of land and natural resources impose themselves as a pervasive system-wide phenomenon which shapes the uncoordinated decisions of individuals into the demographic equilibrium.

Ricardo (1951) extended and elaborated Malthus' notion of demographic equilibrium to a picture of a *stationary state* in which the pressure of capital and labor resources on limited land would force the return to capital, the profit rate, close to zero, and choke off the process of Smithian accumulation. Ricardo's vision rests, like Malthus' on the implicit assumption of diminishing returns to population and capital in the face of limited land resources. But his account of the equalization of profit rates, which underlies the mechanisms that enforce the stationary state, is the same gravitational mechanism we find in Smith. The individual capitalist does not see the rise in rents and in money wages that squeeze his profit rate as connected to his own accumulation. The process of accumulation does not necessarily follow any predetermined path toward the stationary state. Ricardo's arguments are powerful because he shows how *any* path of accumulation will run itself into the stationary state, given only the general phenomenon of diminishing returns associated with limited land resources. In the stationary state itself some capitalists may be making profits and accumulating, while others are making losses and decumulating. Ricardo's stationary state is not a reflection of a microeconomic equilibrium in which each agent finds itself, but a self-organizing state of a complex system that continues to adapt and change, even as it reproduces the stationary state as a macroeconomic average.

Marx

Karl Marx took the Classical political economy of Smith, Malthus, and Ricardo as the basis of his critical reconstruction of the theory of the capitalist economy. Marx instinctively and unquestioningly adopted the mode of argument of the political economists, which sought to discover aggregate regularities in the capitalist economy that did not depend on the detailed behavior of individuals. The power of his methods of analysis, which has been the frequent subject of admiring comment, rests on this foundation. Marx can reach powerful, general, analytical conclusions about the course and patterns of capitalist economic development without limiting himself to particular implausible and limited "models," and without claiming to predict the actual behavior of particular individuals.

Marx brought to political economy the language of "dialectics" that pervaded Continental philosophical thought, particularly through the writing of Hegel, in his youth. In my view, dialectics can be usefully understood as an attempt to find a precise language to discuss the phenomena of system complexity and self-organization.

From one point of view, complex systems are "determined" by the propensities and tendencies of their constituent parts (e.g. the chemical properties of proteins in the cell, or the behavioral tendencies of households and firms in a capitalist economy). But the aggregate behavior of complex systems is far from a simple reflection of these tendencies at the aggregate level. In fact, complex systems paradoxically tend to exhibit features that are in many respects the opposite of the tendencies of their components. The resolute pursuit of profit by individual capitalists, for example, may lead to a falling average rate of profit in the system as a whole. Dialectical language promotes this observation to the (contested) status of a "law."

Despite its features of self-organization, a complex, adaptive system is in a constant process of development and change. Self-organizing aspects of the system emerge because they are independent to a very considerable degree from the detailed function of any particular part of the system. Complex systems tend to be able to continue to function recognizably even when some of their constituent subsystems are disrupted. Randomly wired computers, for example, organize themselves in ways that cannot be destroyed by cutting a few links, while we know that even the smallest failure of a single component completely disables conventional computing machines. Thus the self-organization of a complex system appears to be "over-determined" in dialectical language, in that the destruction of one or even several pathways through which the feature reproduces itself may not succeed in altering the self-organization of the system as a whole.

While complex adaptive systems are "determinate" in the sense that it is in principle possible to trace the interactions among their myriad components that are responsible for their aggregate behavior, they are not "predetermined" in the sense that we can hope to figure out the exact path of their future evolution. Complex systems share this lack of predeterminacy and predictability with chaotic systems, since it arises from the extremely large number of degrees of freedom that characterize both systems. Chaotic systems, however, are so unstable that they break down self-organizing structures very rapidly, while complex systems can sustain self-organizing structures over long periods. Curiously, the disorder of chaotic systems makes them statistically predictable, while complex systems create irregular statistical patterns that are impossible to extrapolate. Dialectics acknowledges this lack of predeterminacy in complex systems by insisting that the future is genuinely open, though constantly being shaped by the actions of constituent particles in the present. This is a key point of difference between the conceptual worlds of equilibrium and self-organizing complex systems. Equilibrium systems tend to return to predetermined states, while complex systems undergo open-ended evolution.

Marx frequently refers to Ricardo, and uses Ricardo's arguments as the basis of his own reformulations of the discoveries of Classical political economy. In part this is due to Marx's appreciation (shared by many other readers) of the analytical power and sharpness of Ricardo's mind. But in substance Marx is a Smithian much more than a Ricardian. The crucial point here is the role of diminishing returns to capital accumulation. Marx shared Smith's view that the essence of capitalism as a social form of organization is its ability to overcome diminishing returns through the widening social division of labor and the technical advances the division of labor makes possible. Marx, in fact, elaborated a powerful systematic account (Marx, 1981, ch. 13) (based on Ricardo's remarkable chapter on Machinery) of the way in which capitalism institutionalizes technical change through the struggles of particular firms to gain cost advantages from new technology. This line of thinking was fundamental to Joseph Schumpeter's work on the dynamics of capitalist economies. But, again, notice that this theory of Marx's is not a set of hypotheses about the specific course of technical change, nor about particular technologies. It is better seen as an account of a tendency of capitalist systems to organize themselves as engines of technical change, whatever the particular technical challenges they face might happen to be historically. Marx, like Smith, sees the essential character of capital accumulation as an ongoing, open-ended, evolutionary process.

Marx also believed that the capitalist system rested on a contradictory and morally unsustainable system of exploitation of labor. Smith is enough of a realist to acknowledge the class basis of capitalist society, but also enthusiastic enough about capitalist process to gloss over the problem of class divisions in the belief that workers will substantively share in the gains of productivity over time. On this point Smith, at least in the context of highly developed capitalist economies, has proved to be right so far. Smith foresees no particular fate for capitalism, unlike Ricardo and Malthus, who forecast the stationary state as a kind of "heat-death" for capital accumulation. For Marx, on the other hand, capitalism as a system would eventually have to evolve to resolve its class contradictions. Complex systems theory suggests that it is very difficult to resolve these speculative historical questions, since there is no way to compress the analysis of a complex system into a model that is any less complex than the system itself.

Classical method

Complex systems pose major challenges to our "common-sense" notions about determinacy, predictability, and stability. It might seem at first that complex systems are inherently invulnerable to systematic analysis. In some respects this is true. We cannot hope to model the future path of a complex system in detail, because of the intractable multiplicity of its degrees of freedom and the paradoxes inherent in its capacity for self-reference and self-reflection. The phenomenon of self-organization, however, opens up a sphere of possible analysis. It is possible to understand the forces that make for the self-organization of a complex system in some dimensions, and to model these limited aspects of the system. Classical political economists' theories of competition, demographic equilibrium, and technical change are good examples of this method. Understanding the self-organizing aspects of complex systems is immensely valuable knowledge, but inevitably frustratingly incomplete. For example, we might be very confident in predicting that insofar as the economy continued to function on the basis of commodity exchange, it will organize itself into markets with prices, and that competitive forces will create weaker or stronger mechanisms of induced technical change. This is a vitally important thing to know about the capitalist economy. On the other hand, it tells us nothing about the details of what products will become leading commodities, where the specific centers and bottlenecks of technical change will emerge, or even how markets will be organized or over what spatial or temporal regions. These are the things we would like to know to make good decisions about education, speculative investments, and public policy.

The self-organization of complex systems thus presents the apparent paradox of promising analytical knowledge about open-ended, evolutionary processes which are inherently unpredictable. The triumph of Classical political economy, in my view, was its uncanny power to discover this type of result. It thus points the way to a solution of a difficult philosophical dilemma. Those who remain committed to the idea of an analytically based social science without adopting the complex systems vision are forced to deny the open-ended, indeterminate character of human social life. These thinkers will force the complexity of social life into simpler forms for the sake of making them amenable to analysis. Those who remain committed to the vision of an open-ended, evolutionary account of human social life without recognizing the phenomenon of self-organization seem condemned to a kind of epistemological nihilism. For them the social world is complex and determinate, but it is impossible to say anything systematic about it. The recognition of self-organization as a pervasive tendency of complex, adaptive systems offers the possibility of discovering and analyzing substantive regularities of complex systems like the economy without hypostatizing them as realized equilibrium states.

Self-organization and equilibrium

In some cases it is possible to study the self-organizing tendency of the economy in terms of homeostatic feedback mechanisms that can be represented by differential equations. For example, it is not hard to represent Malthus' theory of demographic equilibrium in a two-dimensional system of equations involving population and the standard of living, linked by a fertility-mortality relationship on the one hand and a population-productivity relationship on the other. (I will develop this system in detail in Chapter 4.) Mathematicians call the rest point of a set of differential equations an "equilibrium," but I am insisting on a sharp distinction between the concepts of self-organization and equilibrium. This suggests that the term "equilibrium" has different meanings in different contexts, as indeed it does. Mathematicians, physicists, and economists use the term "equilibrium" in significantly different ways.

A very fruitful notion in science is the concept of a *dynamical system*. A list of quantities describing the relevant aspects of a dynamical system at any moment in time constitute its *state*. The collection of all possible states the system might be in constitute the *state space*. For example, we might represent Malthus' system by defining the state of the economy at any moment as its population, productivity, fertility, and mortality. The notion of a dynamical system is that the motion of the system through time is determined by its current state.

Mathematicians call the rest points of a dynamical system (states at which there is no tendency for the system to move) *equilibria*. States that are close to an equilibrium constitute its *neighborhood*. An equilibrium is *locally stable* if the system remains in the neighborhood of the equilibrium whenever it starts in the neighborhood of an equilibrium. An equilibrium is *globally stable* if the system tends to move to a neighborhood of the equilibrium and stay there whatever state it starts from.

A chaotic system is locally unstable but globally stable. The laws of motion of the system prevent it from converging to a particular equilibrium state, but also prevent it from moving very far from its globally stable equilibrium. Such a system restlessly explores a subset of the states in the neighborhood of the globally stable equilibrium (its *attractor*). In this case it is possible to describe the motion of the system statistically, that is, to predict accurately what proportion of time it will spend in any subset of the neighborhood of the globally stable equilibrium it occupies. Malthus' demographic equilibrium is globally stable on his assumptions that fertility increases and mortality decreases with productivity, and that productivity declines with population, but very likely would be locally unstable, with ceaseless small fluctuations in fertility, mortality, population, and productivity.

Physicists use the term "thermodynamic equilibrium" to denote a macroscopic state of a system that tends to reproduce itself, even if at a microscopic scale the system is moving around in the state space. For example, physicists regard the molecules of air in a bicycle tire under pressure as being in an equilibrium state, despite the fact that the individual molecules are constantly moving around and colliding with each other and the walls of the tire. If we open the valve of the tire, however, we create a thermodynamic disequilibrium between the air in the tire and the atmosphere. Thermodynamic or statistical equilibrium represents the tendency for macroscopic variables, such as temperature and pressure, to return to stable states, even though the underlying microscopic state of the system, representing the positions and momenta of individual molecules, is constantly changing. This thermodynamic notion of equilibrium is conceptually very close to the idea of self-organization of a complex system. The orderliness of a thermodynamic system at the aggregate level reflects, however, its complete lack of order at the micro-level. In fact, a basic method for computing the thermodynamic equilibrium of a system is to find the macro-state which is compatible with the greatest degree of disorder at the micro-level, as measured by the *entropy* of the system. In many cases the micro-level disorder is the result of the unstable chaotic motion of the corresponding mathematical dynamical system.

Curiously, economists have begun to adopt the thermodynamic notion of equilibrium as a conceptual tool only recently (see, e.g. Foley, 1994). The traditional economic notion of equilibrium requires each household and firm in the economy to be in equilibrium at a microscopic level in order for the economy itself to be in equilibrium. The orderliness of an economic equilibrium system at the macro-economic level is a reflection of its complete orderliness at the micro-economic level. The traditional Walrasian conception of economic equilibrium has zero entropy: it is completely orderly at the micro-level.

Self-organized, complex, adaptive systems, on the other hand, cannot typically be regarded as being in equilibrium either in the physical or traditional economic senses. Self-organization cannot occur in a stable dynamical system, which tends to collapse all structures into the stable equilibrium state. Self-organization is also unsustainable in a completely locally unstable and therefore chaotic dynamical system. Any embryonic structure in such a system is quickly dissipated. Self-organizing structures are characteristic of systems that are mathematically neither locally stable nor locally unstable, which can sustain and reproduce recognizable structures over long periods of time. Like thermodynamic equilibrium systems, complex, self-organizing systems stably reproduce patterns in some aggregates, even though the underlying state-space dynamics are locally unstable. In contrast to thermodynamic equilibrium systems, however, complex, self-organized systems remain far from their maximum-entropy equilibrium states. Their self-organization is a sign of this thermodynamic disequilibrium: the reproduction of their self-organized structures is incompatible with the complete disorderliness maximum entropy demands.

Complex, self-organized systems are, well..., complex. Some subsystems of a complex, self-organized system can be in thermodynamic equilibrium, even though the system as a whole is organized far from equilibrium. Our blood, for example, reaches thermodynamic equilibrium at a measurable temperature, even though it circulates as part of a self-organized non-equilibrium system, our bodies, that maintains itself at a different temperature from its environment. Thus we can see several different types of order in complex, self-organized systems. Some parts may be in economic or thermodynamic equilibrium, which will reveal itself in an examination of their microscopic behavior. Self-organizing structures reflected in some aggregates reproduce themselves in an orderly fashion. But the system as a whole is in a constant process of development.

The El Farol problem

An example of Arthur's (1994) may help to fix the phenomenon of self-organization in our understanding. Arthur considers a local bar (or pub) ("El Farol," in his original telling) which is the kind of place that is fun to visit when it has no more than 60 people in it. When the crowd gets much bigger than 60, it is noisy and boring. The bar has several hundred regular customers who like to go there. On any given night each regular has to decide whether or not to go. Arthur supposes that each regular has a whole group of models that are intended to predict how many people will be in the bar on any given night. These models use data on the actual attendance at the bar over the past as an input. Different regulars may have different models, or in some cases the models may overlap. At each moment in time each regular customer adopts the model in his or her group of models that has best fit the data over the past. If that model predicts attendance less than 60, the customer goes to the bar that night; if it predicts attendance greater than 60, the customer stays home. In simulations the attendance at the bar hovers around 60 customers each night, which reflects a strong self-organizing tendency of this system. But there is no equilibrium in the micro-state which describes the model and behavior of each particular customer. The customers ceaselessly change the models they use, and their individual pattern of attendance does not follow a maximum-entropy statistical law. The system as a whole is far from equilibrium, despite the fact that attendance is extremely regular. One can imagine that similar forces might be at work behind many social phenomena, such as the distribution of taxis in large cities, the size and growth rates of urban centers, the outbreak of wars, and the like. It is possible to see why Arthur's system self-organizes in this dimension. If the number of customers attending rises for several nights much above 60, for example, those who attend must have received wrong predictions from their models, and will tend to shift to different models, typically, but not necessarily, to models that tend to predict a higher attendance at the bar and hence to discourage their users from going. A symmetric dynamic will follow a series of nights when the attendance is well below 60, due to the disappointment of those who stayed home when they would rather have gone out. This very general feedback mechanism stabilizes the number of customers attending, even without any tendency for the models or the behavior of individual customers to stabilize (or to converge to some "correct," or "perfect foresight" model). The analogy with the Classical theory of competition is also clear. The individual profit-seeking capitalists of the Classical story do not settle on one equilibrium plan or strategy. Like the customers in Arthur's bar model, they very well may be ceaselessly seeking new ways to look at the economy and to discover profit opportunities or recognize markets in decline. But despite their failure to reach any equilibrium in their own behavior, they tend to equalize profit rates.

The El Farol problem is closely linked to the "minority game," where the high payoff is in choosing a strategy different from the strategy chosen by the majority of players. Versions of the minority games appear in many different political economic contexts. The Classical theory of competition is based on the insight that a capitalist wants to invest in sectors where capital is scarce. The El Farol problem is also closely linked to John Maynard Keynes' model of asset markets as a "beauty contest" in which the prize goes to the player who best anticipates the average opinion of all the other players (Keynes, 1936).

Political economy and self-organization

From the point of view of political economy the phenomenon of self-organization opens up important methodological perspectives. The difficulty with the equilibrium point of view, whether thermodynamic or economic, is that it is forced to associate strong micro-level structure, in the case of economic equilibrium, or the maximization of micro-level disorder, in the case of thermodynamic equilibrium, with observed aggregate regularities. The equilibrium point of view is, in this sense, methodologically too strong. It can explain aggregate regularity only by positing a corresponding micro-level equilibrium or chaos. These micro-level predictions are often incorrect, leaving the equilibrium theorist either with the need to scrap the theory altogether, or to insist against the evidence on micro-level equilibrium that is simply not present in reality. The recognition of the phenomenon of self-organization can avoid these pitfalls, allowing the political economist to investigate the dynamics of self-reproducing structures in economic life without projecting them inappropriately onto the complex and evolving micro-level behavior of households and firms.

But the self-organizing point of view raises its own methodological problems. The success of the method depends on the power of the tendencies towards self-organization to operate over a very wide range of micro-level situations. Conventional economic modeling tends, on the contrary, to demonstrate the tendency of a *specific* micro-level equilibrium to give rise to an aggregate regularity. Any particular model of this kind inevitably raises the question of how general the demonstrated result is. When we demonstrate equalization of the profit rate in a specific model (assuming, e.g. a given set of commodities and given technology), how do we argue for the generalizability of the result to a wide, ill-determined set of possible environments (such as changing commodity space or technologies)? Certainly demonstrating the result in particular models is a necessary first step, but the longer-run goal is to get insights into the behavior of a large class of systems, of which the model represents only a part.

This methodological problem creates a gap between those who, in the name of scientific skepticism and conservatism, accept results only in the domain in which they have been demonstrated, and those who, in the search for insight and understanding, want to project or generalize results demonstrated in a narrow domain to a wider domain on the basis of intuition or instinct. This division, which characterizes the dialectic of scientific knowledge, becomes particularly acute in the study of complex, self-organizing systems. Self-organization may be meaningful only in complex, nonequilibrium systems that are difficult or impossible to represent in general, closed, tractable, mathematical models. It may be possible to demonstrate the self-organization only by simulating highly simplified and abstract models of the system in question on a computer. In this case all we have, in the skeptic's eyes, is a collection of specific examples, similar to anecdotes. The self-organization demonstrated may be due either to the general structure of the system (i.e. if we can even agree on what it is), or to specific, possibly obscure, peculiarities of the cases simulated.

The Classical political economists and Marx worked in an intellectual milieu that was much more sympathetic to speculation and extrapolation from example than many scientists are today. Still, even the strict constructionists of the present economic mandarinate accept at some level or other the general validity of the Classical theory of competition, even if only as a heuristic to guide the formulation of specific, narrow models. There is some hope that the Classical modes of argument and results can bolster the investigation of the economy as a complex, self-organizing system far from equilibrium.

From Malthus to Darwin to Kauffman

How anachronistic is it to suggest that the Classical political economists conceived of the capitalist economy as what we would now call a complex, adaptive, self-organizing system? On the one hand, the mathematical language of complex systems theory is the product of the last twenty or thirty years (though some mathematicians were thinking about this type of system before). On the other, there is a clearly traceable intellectual path from the Classical political economists to contemporary complex systems theory. Curiously enough, this path does not run directly through economic analysis, but through biology.

The development of mathematics in the seventeenth and eighteenth centuries was closely connected with the development of astronomy and physics. This era of physics aimed at deriving closed-form expressions for the behavior of relatively simple systems, like the planetary system, from a small number of fundamental laws, like the law of gravity. The need for such closed-form solutions (actually approximations) arose from the primitive level of computational methods available, basically paper and pencil in the hands of a human being. (Newton, Gauss, and other great mathematical minds of this period spent what in retrospect appears to be an astonishing amount of time and energy carrying out elaborate computations of planetary orbits by hand, an activity that strangely enough seems to have been the foundation of their scientific prestige.) The paradigmatic system in this era was the clock, a mechanical device maintained in regular stable motion by simple feedback mechanisms.

It is striking how little of this vision of a clockwork universe finds expression in the writing of the Classical political economists. As we have seen, Smith's vision of the capitalist economy, while it included the notion that the economy was in some dimensions self-regulating (if not self-organizing), was far from mechanical, and has closer affinities to living, developing and growing biological systems. Malthus advertises the "mathematical" character of his argument, but his mathematics turns out not to be a formal equilibrium system akin to the derivations of planetary orbits by celestial mechanics, but the demonstration of the asymptotic incompatibility of an arithmetically growing series to represent food production and a geometrically growing series to represent population. The explanation may very well be that the Classical political economists did not know enough of the advanced mathematics of their time to be influenced by it. But the Classical political economists, who were widely read and exhibited curiosity about everything under the sun, don't seem to have been very interested in the mathematics available to them. An exception is Marx, who thought rather hard about the philosophical basis of the differential calculus (see Marx, 1983). The Classical political economists do not seem to have been attracted by the idea of representing the economy as a clockwork system governed by a simple principle of maximization or minimization like the principle of least action that unifies classical mechanics.

Statistical equilibrium concepts in physics emerged in the 1850s, after the work of all the Classical political economists except Marx (if one counts him as a Classical political economist). Statistical ideas originated in the empirical investigation of social phenomena in the first half of the nineteenth century, and are one important path by which the concepts of social science influenced the development of formal systems theory and the "harder" sciences (see Porter, 1986; Stigler, 1986). The mathematical roots of complex system theory lie in the rigorous investigation of the foundations of statistical mechanics, and the consequent discovery that systems with many degrees of freedom, even when they are governed by simple laws at the microscopic level, are capable of a bewilderingly rich range of aggregate behavior.

But there is another, more direct, and better known path connecting Classical political economy with modern complex systems theory, which runs through biology rather than physics. Charles Darwin's speculations on natural selection began from Malthus' image of the struggle for survival implicit in the relentless pressure of human population on food resources. Darwin formulated the evolution of species as the outcome of this struggle for survival in the presence of random mutations. The evolutionary process is a paradigm of a complex system. The principles that ultimately govern it at the microscopic level, mutation and fitness, are simple to state and understand, but their consequences on the macroscopic level are varied, path-dependent, and open-ended. Evolution is one of the central strands of modern complex systems thinking.

Economists, in the meantime, developed a curious schizophrenia in their thinking about the economy. With the invention of marginalism in the 1880s, the mechanical mathematics of least action, already on the wane in the physical sciences, arrived in economic thinking with a vengeance (see Mirowski, 1992). Marginalist economists came increasingly to formulate models of the economy so as to be amenable to closed-form analytical solution in imitation of the physics of the eighteenth century. But at the same period the biological metaphor of evolution also appealed to many economists as the natural conceptual foundation for economics. The Institutionalist movement in economics, following Thorstein Veblen, attempted to find a scholarly discipline on the evolutionary metaphor. Alfred Marshall's attempted synthesis of Classical political economy, marginalism, and institutionalism unfortunately degenerated into a complacent neoclassical orthodoxy whose intellectual heritage still weighs heavily on economics. But Marshall was strongly drawn to the evolutionary model and to the idea that biology, not physics, was the appropriate model for economics. (For some reason the notion that economics might be better regarded as the conceptual model for physics or biology has not had much of a hearing.) Allyn Young, a highly respected American economist who had a foot in both the neoclassical and institutionalist camps, puts forward similar ideas (see Young, 1927). The sociology of American economics in the first half of the twentieth century is the story of an academic duel to the death between the neoclassical and institutionalist schools, a duel in which the neoclassical school won a Pyrrhic victory through wielding the weapon of mathematical sophistication.

Marshall and Young exemplify another connection between complex systems theory and economics. The marginalist resurrection of eighteenth century celestial mechanics as a mathematical model of the economy is incapable of dealing with the phenomenon of increasing returns, a technical theme of great importance to Marshall and Young. At one level this difficulty appears in the theory of competition: with increasing returns one firm tends to dominate each industry, thus frustrating the achievement of the static equilibrium of marginal cost and benefit that is the centerpiece of the neoclassical story. But when we look at increasing returns from a dynamic point of view, we see that it leads directly to the main themes of complexity theory. Increasing returns destroys the local stability of the neoclassical equilibrium, but it is evident that firms cannot grow indefinitely large, and that countervailing non-linear forces must come into play to regulate the evolution of the system even if competition cannot enforce the neoclassical marginal equalities. An increasing returns economy (as Brian Arthur and others have emphasized) is inherently open-ended and path-dependent, like the evolution of species (where a fitness advantage operates analogously to competitive advantage with economic increasing returns). This line of thought leads forward through the ideas of Herbert Simon (e.g. Simon, 1992) to the economic version of complex systems theory, which sees the economy as a complex, adaptive system governed by increasing returns. It is not hard to see that it also leads back to the Classical political economic theory of competition, which posits the self-regulatory character of an economy without insisting on achieved marginalist equilibrium.

Complex systems theory proper emerged in the 1960s and 1970s in the convergence of these intellectual developments in physics, biology, mathematics, computer science, and economics. Physicists and mathematicians such as Erwin Schrödinger, Alan Turing, and John von Neumann turned their attention to various aspects of the problem of understanding the reproduction and structure of living organisms. The development of population genetics revealed its close relations to dynamical systems theory and began to force theoretical biologists to consider the abstract nature of evolution as a system. These intellectual efforts produced an explosion of particular models of complex, self-organizing systems, such as von Neumann's cellular automaton, which made the distinctive properties of these non-equilibrium but organized systems vivid and inescapable. Biologists like Stuart Kauffman discovered deep structural similarities between self-organization in complex systems as diverse as the living cell, the ecology of species and the capitalist economy (see Mirowski, 2001).

Perhaps I speak from a biased point of view, but it seems to me that the master principle at work in these developments has been the power of the economic metaphor in the "hard" sciences, not the influence of physical or biological metaphors in economics. As human beings we have a direct existential experience of the operation of the capitalist economy as a complex, adaptive system, which informs our imagination in dealing with other complex systems in physics and biology. In this sense I would argue for the direct relevance of Classical political economy to the emergence of the contemporary complex systems vision, and claim a significant, perhaps even dominant, intellectual ancestry for the Classical political economists.

Classical themes

In succeeding chapters I will discuss some key themes of the Classical political economists: distribution and productivity, the impact of limited natural resources on capitalist economic development, and the determinants of world population.

Distribution and productivity

Malthus and Ricardo foresaw a future for capitalist economic development very different in terms of the distribution of income between classes and productivity of inputs to production from what has actually happened. They believed that the real wage of workers would not change very much in the course of capitalist economic development. Though they correctly foresaw that output would grow substantially through capital accumulation, they emphasized a pattern of overall decline in labor productivity, the ratio of output to labor input, due to diminishing returns with limited land and natural resources. They thought that the same diminishing returns would lead to a limited rise in land productivity, the ratio of output to land input. With a decline in labor productivity and a more or less constant wage, the share of wages in output would grow, squeezing profits and the profit share in output to zero. In Ricardo's stationary state, the whole surplus product of the economy above the subsistence wage level takes the form of rent.

In fact, the broad patterns of capitalist development have been dramatically different. The single most persistent and important feature of capitalist development has been the tendency for labor productivity to rise continuously at a significant rate. If this increase in labor productivity had been accompanied by a stagnant level of the real wage, the wage share would have fallen dramatically, but in fact the real wage has tended, roughly speaking, to grow in proportion to labor productivity over the long run, so that the wage share in output has remained roughly constant. It is difficult to overstate the historical importance of these two factors in shaping the social and political development of capitalist society. While diminishing returns to land and natural resources have created occasional bottlenecks for capital accumulation, on the whole the productivity of land and natural resources has also grown very rapidly, in sharp contrast to Ricardo's and Malthus' vision of diminishing returns. In fact there seems to be little evidence of an increase in rent as a share of output.

Smith, in contrast, argues for a sustained increase in labor productivity through the widening of the division of labor. In the place of Ricardo and Malthus' principle of diminishing returns Smith puts a "virtuous cycle" in which capital accumulation increases the scale of production, which makes a wider division of labor possible through technical change, which in turn further encourages capital accumulation. Smith is characteristically vague about the tendency of wages, though he is clear that rapid capital accumulation tends to pull wages above the costs of reproducing labor at a subsistence level. He is perhaps inconsistent in his treatment of land, natural resources, and rent, since alongside his vision of the positive feedback of capital accumulation to the division of labor he pictures a stationary state (e.g. in his comments on China) in terms similar to Ricardo's.

Marx follows Smith rather than Malthus and Ricardo in his analysis of labor and land productivity. Marx emphasizes the historically unprecedented technological progressiveness of the capitalist mode of production. The organization of the exploitation of labor through competing capitalist firms creates both the incentive and the ability for capitalists to discover and implement new technologies in an effort to reduce costs. This turns capitalist production into an engine of technical change. Marx argues that Malthus and Ricardo, in emphasizing diminishing returns to fixed land and natural resources, lost sight of the historical genius of capitalism, which is to overcome technical barriers to production. But Marx could not see any systematic reason for the wage to rise along with labor productivity in the course of capital accumulation. In the earlier phase of his study of economics he adopted a version of Malthus' and Ricardo's theory of the subsistence wage. In conjunction with rapidly rising labor productivity, a stagnating or slowly growing real wage leads to a fall in the wage share in output. This picture was politically congenial to Marx. If capitalism were to follow a path of rising labor productivity and a stagnating real wage, it would rapidly face a revolutionary situation, in which workers, conscious of their ability to produce a high standard of living, and systematically frustrated in their efforts to participate in the fruits of high productivity, would insist on taking control of the productive system.

Around 1860, as Marx was working on preparing *Capital* for publication, a tendency for real wages to rise in Britain, which he regarded as the bellwether of the capitalist nations, became apparent. I think this caused Marx considerable dismay, and perhaps a loss of confidence in his revolutionary project. He began to introduce a more nuanced and complex theory of wages and workers' standard of living into his economic analysis, emphasizing the constancy or fall in the value of labor-power (which correlates with the wage share in output) rather than a constancy in real wages in the course of capital accumulation, and to refer to the "relative" immiserization of workers, rather than their absolute impoverishment by capital accumulation.

But from the Classical political economy point of view the rise in wages poses an intriguing puzzle. Why should workers, relatively disorganized, easily divided, and constantly threatened by an influx of competition from various reserves of labor, be able to secure a rise in real wages in bargaining with a prosperous, politically unified capitalist class, even in a context of rising labor productivity? We are still far from understanding the complexities of the capitalist labor market, though some features of it have become clearer over the years. The labor market is highly segmented, so that the competitive pressure of reserves exerts itself only fitfully and gradually on specific wage bargains. The acquisition of skills, licensing and unions, the costs and risks of migration, linguistic and cultural differences, all present barriers to competition in the labor market. The rise in average wages that has taken place over the course of capitalist economic development has been extremely uneven. Both on the national and world scale disparities in workers' income are just as notable as the increase in the average level of the wage.

Recent work by Duménil and Lévy (1995), revisiting from the perspective of Marx's theory of induced technical change the study of technical progress undertaken by earlier writers (Kennedy, 1964; Drandakis and Phelps, 1966; Shah and Desai, 1981; van der Ploeg, 1987) suggests some new approaches to the problem of distribution and growth. From a Classical/Marxist point of view accumulation in capitalist economies fundamentally arises from profits, so that the rate of growth of capital, the most important determinant of the demand for labor-power, is closely and positively correlated with the profit rate. The profit rate in turn can be viewed as the product of the "productivity of capital," the ratio of the value of output to the value of capital, and the profit share in output (transformed versions of Marx's "organic composition of capital" and "rate of surplus value"). The profit rate in rapidly developing capitalist economies tends to be high enough to absorb local reserves of labor and create upward pressure on the wage and the wage share. One version of this type of account (the "profit squeeze" theories) sees the rise in the wage share, which corresponds to a fall in the profit share, as equilibrating the system by lowering the rate of accumulation to equal the rate of growth of the supply of labor-power. Robert Solow's influential model of growth reflects these ideas, which have the implication that the rate of growth of the capitalist economy is ultimately limited by the rate of growth of labor-supply.

Duménil and Lévy remind us that the rate of growth of the productivity of capital is also influenced by distribution. This point can be made in a number of modeling contexts, but at its root depends on the simple observation that the contribution of any input-saving innovation to raising the profit rate is proportional to the share of the input in cost. When the wage share is high, capitalists have a strong incentive to find labor-saving technical changes, and will be glad to implement them even if they cost something in terms of increased capital inputs. When the wage share is low, on the other hand, the incentives to technical change shift relatively toward capital-saving innovations.

This observation suggests, first of all, that the remarkable record of capitalism in fostering rising labor productivity is closely connected to a *high* share of wages in output. Attempts to bolster the profit rate by lowering the wage share through government policy, for example, have the side effect of lowering the rate of growth of labor productivity.

The implications of recognizing the dependence of the bias of technical change between labor- and capital-saving innovations on the share of wages and profit in output go significantly further. The profit rate can stabilize only when the rate of change of capital productivity is zero, no matter what the rate of growth of change of labor productivity may be. The mechanism of induced technical change tends to keep the wage share at the level at which the rate of change of capital productivity is zero. The *level* of capital productivity then must adjust to make the profit rate and rate of accumulation adapt to the availability of labor-power.

Thus, this general approach offers a powerful explanation of the characteristic (but unexpected) pattern of capitalist economic development. The wage share in advanced capitalist countries has to be high enough to induce a relatively low rate of change in capital productivity on average, and variations in the input-saving bias of technical change tend to stabilize the wage share at this level. The tendency for wages and labor productivity to rise steadily and roughly in proportion are a reflection of what Marx called the "revolutionary" character of capitalist production. This works because capitalism, in contrast to other modes of production, simultaneously gives capitalists control over technology, the means, through profits, of implementing new technologies, and a fierce competitive motive to cut costs of production.

To the degree that capitalist economies self-organize toward a state of zero rate of change of capital productivity through a high and stable wage share, the wage share itself becomes insulated in the long run from factors influencing both the supply and demand for labor-power, such as the rate of growth of the potential labor force, or the proportion of profits capitalists accumulate. These forces of supply and demand in the labor market regulate the level of capital productivity to keep accumulation in equilibrium with the potential supply of labor. Attempts through government policy to raise the wage share, for example, will tend to be frustrated by a process in which the adoption of labor-saving technical changes is accelerated, the productivity of capital falls, and the rate of accumulation stagnates.

This approach to the theory of capital also has implications for some of the most vexed and puzzling problems in economic theory. Neoclassical and marginalist economists want to see the *value* of capital as a measure of its real productivity in use-value terms. This makes no sense from a Classical/Marxian point of view, which sees the only "use-value" of capital as its potential to save wage costs by substituting for labor. Following Piero Sraffa's brilliant critical investigations, twentieth-century followers of the Classical economists showed that the neoclassical interpretation of the value of capital as representing some real productive factor is untenable, and that there is no reason to think that in general firms react to a lower profit rate by adopting more "capital-intensive" techniques of production. The induced technical change theory, however, explains regular tendencies in the ratio of the value of output to the value of capital not as the reflection of an underlying "production function" linking capital intensity to labor productivity, but as the outcome of a dynamic feedback process motivated by and responsive to the ratio of the value of output to the value of capital. From this point of view the real force regulating the capital-intensity of capitalist production is the profit rate and its tendency to stabilize, not an underlying "real productivity" of capital.

Land, the environment, and production

We now recognize that the emission of carbon dioxide and other "greenhouse" gases into the atmosphere as a byproduct of economic production will lead to pervasive and, in many ways, harmful changes in the earth's climate through "global warming." The design, evaluation, and implementation of public policy to mitigate global warming pose important questions for economic analysis. Because global warming unfolds on such a long timescale, from two hundred to four hundred years, corresponding to the half-life of carbon dioxide in the atmosphere, the long-period analytical methods of Classical political economy promise to be particularly relevant in this area.

In principle the world can control the emission of greenhouse gases either directly by legally enforced mandates on emissions, or indirectly through the establishment of financial incentives for emissions reduction. The design, implementation, and enforcement of mandated emission controls are probably beyond our capability given the global extent and complexity of the problem. The Kyoto protocols envision a system of tradeable emissions permits. While the details of the initial distribution and exact scope of the permit system are still unresolved, the scheme would require existing and new emissions sources to be licensed by acquiring these permits. Since the permits will be scarce, they will generate royalties (so many dollars per ton of carbon dioxide or its equivalent emitted per year). From the point of view of emitters, the permits will put a price on greenhouse gas emissions as an input to production on the same footing with capital, labor, and other priced natural resources like oil.

If indeed the uncontrolled emission of greenhouse gases will impose a net cost on economic production (through the balance of increased storm damage, flooding of valuable land, increased agricultural productivity in high latitudes, and the host of other impacts of world climate change) then it should be possible to design a mitigation scheme which improves the economic welfare of both current and future generations. The mitigation of global warming, from an economic point of view, poses the problem of distributing a net benefit to different countries and generations, not the problem of allocating a net cost, as politicians and diplomats tend to see it. Without a clearer understanding of the exact economic consequences of mitigation schemes like the emissions permit system the world may very well miss its chance for their enormous potential benefits.

Raising the price of greenhouse gas emissions as an input to production may in the short run induce some modest substitution of other inputs for emissions. But the possibilities of substitution in the case of already-existing power plants and transportation networks is limited. It seems likely that over the many decades involved in the global warming scenario the most important impact of emissions charges will be their influence on patterns of technical change through research and development. The difficulty this poses for economic analysis is that we do not have a very good understanding of the economics of long-run technical change, nor very good data from which to extrapolate over such a long time scale.

The Classical/Marxian theory of induced technical change as an explanation of the evolution of labor and capital productivity and the wage share offers a promising analytical approach to these problems. By extending the analysis to three inputs to production, labor, capital, and land (representing the capacity of the environment to absorb the byproducts of production such as greenhouse gas emissions), we can study the paths the world economy will follow with and without the pricing of scarce environmental resources like the atmosphere. In addition to labor and capital productivity, we now take account of environmental productivity and its changes through time.

A system of environmental resource pricing creates the same feedback between the share of output cost represented by the environment and technical change that favors the environment as is already present between the wage share and labor productivity. This feedback induces on average over time a rate of increase in environmental productivity that equals the rate of increase in output, thus stabilizing (though not eliminating) the stress production puts on the environment.

Without a system of environmental resource pricing, on the other hand, the analysis suggests a path of development that has quite disastrous consequences not just for the environment, but for the basic mechanisms of capitalist distribution. In the absence of explicit environmental resource pricing, firms will appropriate some of the value of the scarce environment in the form of profit. Since there is no change in the incentive to invest in environment-saving technical change, firms will instead shift their investment towards capital-saving technical change. Eventually, in these scenarios, the wage share falls so low that the historical tendency of capitalist production to raise labor productivity is reversed. The incentives of the system wind up raising the stress on the environment without limit, and shifting distribution sharply against wages and in favor of profits.

We cannot quantify the magnitude of these effects or the exact time scale on which they might unfold without a better understanding of the exact dynamics of induced technical change than we have at the present time. But this line of thinking emphasizes the fateful importance of the decisions the world faces in relation to systems of environmental control.

Population

One of the most striking differences between the Classical political economy tradition and neoclassical and marginalist economics is the treatment of human population. The Classical political economists universally presumed that the size and growth of the population were a reflection of economic development and performance, that is, "endogenous" in the jargon of economic model-building. People are a by-product of economic activity in this way of looking at things. Marginalist economics, on the other hand, has a strong tendency to view the population as "exogenous," with economic development shaping itself to the limits set by population.

One might suppose that this shift in point of view was a response to new empirical data that called the Classical notions into question, but, as far as I can tell, this is not the case. Neoclassical demographic economics continues to pursue the question of economic determinants of fertility and mortality, and finds strong confirmation of the fundamental Classical insights in modern patterns of population growth and movement. Demography, however, has been marginalized and demoted to a respected but minor place in the neoclassical pantheon, along with locational economics, economic history, and the history of economics. I would suggest that what motivates this changed attitude toward population on the part of neoclassical orthodoxy is its attachment to a particular philosophical view of welfare economics based on its subjective and individual theory of value. Neoclassical economics sees economic value as expressing the ability of commodities to satisfy individual, subjective desires. Neoclassical welfare economics justifies the operation of the market as optimizing the satisfaction of individual, subjective desires, and evaluates public policies by analyzing their impact on individual subjective well-being. This philosophical approach to welfare economics and policy evaluation, enshrined in the discourse of consumers' surplus and Pareto-efficiency, only makes sense if the population of subjective individuals who are the focus of the analysis is given independently of the economic activity and policies being considered. If economic policy has the effect of increasing or diminishing the population itself, the analysis faces the insoluble problem of evaluating the welfare of non-existent individual consumers, either those who exist only as a consequence of the policy measure, or those who will not exist because of the policy measure. Serious attempts to resolve these questions have only revealed their fundamental intractability. Taking the population as exogenous to economic policy and development is a way of avoiding these awkward questions.

In the last chapter of this book I return to the Classical political economists' view that population, in this case world population, is governed by laws that arise in the economic sphere itself. Malthus and Ricardo argued that in the long run human populations would reach a *demographic equilibrium* through rising mortality induced by hunger and disease as a result of diminishing returns to labor in the face of limited land and natural resources. This analysis has proved to be spectacularly wrong as far as the actual history of world population in the last two centuries goes, but is still an immensely popular vehicle for contemporary anxieties about overpopulation and resource limits to growth.

I argue that Malthus proposed a viable method of equilibrium analysis, but reached flawed conclusions because of his uncritical acceptance of key assumptions about the response of fertility and mortality to rising income, and the relation between population and productivity. Malthus assumes that the difference between fertility and mortality rises with income (largely as a result of higher standards of living reducing infant mortality), but we now know that sustained increases in income lower fertility even faster than mortality. Thus there are two demographic equilibria: a low income, Malthusian, equilibrium at which high fertility is balanced by high mortality; and a high income, Smithian, equilibrium at which low mortality is balanced by low fertility induced by a high standard of living.

Malthus probably would have rejected the Smithian equilibrium, if he had considered it seriously, on the grounds that in the presence of diminishing returns, that is, falling productivity with increasing population, the Smithian equilibrium is unstable. For example, if the population were at the Smithian equilibrium level, an accidental increase in the population would lower productivity and income, which would raise fertility, and reinforce the increase in population, pushing the system away from, not back toward, the Smithian equilibrium.

But if the relation between population and productivity is positive, rather than negative, that is, if an increase in population *raises* productivity, the Smithian equilibrium is stable. In this case, a positive shock to the population will raise standards of living, and drive fertility below mortality, leading to a decrease in population back toward the equilibrium level. Smith argued that there is a positive association between population and productivity because of the effect of the increasing division of labor with increasing population. If this Smithian effect outweighs the diminishing returns to limited land and natural resources, which seems to be the case at present for the world economy, the Smithian demographic equilibrium at a relatively high income and low mortality is stable. If the historical association between world population and world output reflects the structural effects of the division of labor, and current national relations of fertility to income continue to hold, this Smithian equilibrium will occur at a population about 25 percent higher than the current world population, and a world average income also about 25 percent higher than current world income.

In fact, it would be very difficult for world population to reach the Malthusian equilibrium (which is also stable), unless diminishing returns (say, in the form of environmental degradation) accelerated so rapidly as to overwhelm the effects of technical progress based in the widening division of labor.

The prospect of a world Smithian demographic equilibrium has comforting aspects on average, in that it offers the hope of managing environmental and resource problems in a context of stable population, and of productivity levels high enough to provide a secure and moderately comfortable standard of life. But all the signs are that the distribution of income and fertility at the Smithian equilibrium will be highly unequal. If so, we face a future polarized between advanced capitalist countries with high incomes, but aging and shrinking populations due to low fertility, and poorer, low productivity countries with young and growing populations due to high fertility. These sharp divisions will motivate trade in people, through the conventional paths of migration and the newer paths of adoption, surrogate parenting, and technological management of fertility.

Caveat lector

The critical reader, such as Alexander J. Julius or Fabio Petri, who brought the following issues to my attention in comments on an earlier version of this book, may see a gap between the methodological claims of this chapter and the examples presented in the rest of the book. It would be more methodologically consistent if the examples explicitly employed a simulation methodology showing that disaggregated agent-based models can exhibit the self-organizing tendencies of the capitalist economy addressed. In fact, the analyses in these chapters are based on differential equations linking aggregate, or macroscopic, variables, and study the equilibria of these systems of equations and their stability.

To some degree this reflects the transitional state of my thinking about political economy, and I can only beg the reader's indulgence to fill this methodological gap. But I think a strong case can be made that agent-based disaggregated models of capitalist competition, innovation, and population change can be constructed that will exhibit the self-organizing tendencies I point to. I invite interested readers to pursue this positive research program. I feel confident, however, that the results reached in these chapters are faithful to the Classical vision on the one hand, and consistent with a complex systems vision of the evolution of the capitalist economy on the other.

Humanity's struggle to control its fate

One way of looking at human history sees it as a continuing collective struggle of humankind to control its fate. The development of nuclear weapons in the past century and the emergence of global environmental threats from production, the implications of genetic engineering, and revolutions in information and communications technology, are the arenas in which this struggle has unfolded in our time.

We face a basic difficulty in controlling our collective fate that humankind is an assembly of individuals whose actions interact in complex ways to form an aggregate outcome. Attempts to solve human problems directly, say, through the invention of new medical or agricultural technologies turn out to have very different consequences as they play out through these complex interactions from the intentions of their promoters. We are only beginning to appreciate the implications of the complexity of human society for these problems.

Theory suggests that it is impossible to control complex, adaptive, self-organizing systems by directing the behavior of the individual entities that comprise them. Traditional conceptions of social policy, on the other hand, depend precisely on an ability to link individual behavior and aggregate outcomes. The methods of Classical political economy offer some hope of surmounting this apparent dilemma. We may be able to design systems that influence the self-organization of society as a complex, adaptive system in particular dimensions, even though we must give up any hope of stabilizing the actual evolution of the system in the hope of attaining once and for all such goals as justice and equality.

I would argue, in fact, that there is much to be gained from this shift in understanding. We avoid the Scylla of utopian fantasies of an end to the dialectical historical development of human societies, which, in the complex systems view, will continue indefinitely. But we also elude the Charybdis of conservative complacency in the face of the very real moral and social problems capitalist society creates and reproduces. What we need is a better understanding of the processes of self-organization that are amenable to our influence.

2   Innovative capitalism and the distribution of income

Contemporary industrial capitalist economies have come to expect consistent significant increases in labor productivity, and a roughly proportional sharing of productivity gains between labor and capital incomes. This expectation is the ground on which much of the political economic drama in these societies plays out. These presumptions are so strong that even relatively small variations in the rate of growth of labor productivity or the wage share in national income are the object of intense scrutiny and debate.

These features of contemporary capitalism would have surprised Thomas Malthus and David Ricardo. They believed strongly in the pervasive importance of diminishing returns to labor and capital with capital accumulation in the face of fixed land resources, and thus would have expected advanced industrial capitalist societies to confront a chronically diminishing, rather than a consistently rising, average productivity of labor. They also saw no sustained basis on which the majority workers could bargain for higher (real) wages in the face of pervasive competitive pressures from overpopulation and immigration.

Karl Marx, on the other hand, foresaw the tendency for capitalism to be a technologically progressive mode of production, with pervasive pressures toward labor-saving innovation in production (Marx, 1976, ch. 12; 1981, Part Three). Ricardo had shown (in his chapter on Machinery) that competitive pressure on individual capitalists to lower costs could lead to a general increase in labor productivity through the substitution of machinery for labor, but seems to have regarded this process as offering only a temporary relief from the pressure of diminishing returns to both capital and labor due to limited land resources. Marx developed this mechanism of induced innovation into a general theory of the tendency of capitalist production to increase labor productivity through the replacement of "living" by "dead" labor, that is the displacement of workers by machines. Through this process Marx saw capitalism as fulfilling its historic mission of developing the forces of production to the point where age-old problems of material scarcity could be eliminated.

In his early writings Marx shared Malthus' and Ricardo's pessimism about the ability of workers to achieve substantial increases in wages within the framework of capitalist social relations, though he emphasized different mechanisms as being responsible. If labor productivity had risen continuously without a proportional rise in wages, capitalist society would soon have faced the revolutionary crisis Marx pinned his hopes on. A constantly growing disparity between the productive power of labor and the standard of living of workers would provide a powerful impetus to the project of socializing the surplus product. Bourgeois society could absorb the rapidly growing social surplus only through a constant increase in conspicuous capitalist consumption, which would reinforce the social resentments latent in the class divisions of the society, and make the stabilization of democratic political institutions problematic. A socialist regime coming to power under these circumstances would find it relatively easy to arrange for a steady rise in workers' standard of living from a very low base, on the basis of a high productivity of labor. Both the motivation for and the feasibility of socialist revolution would have grown had the pattern of rising labor productivity and stagnant wages Marx foresaw in his early writings come to pass. Even as Marx was preparing his critique of political economy for publication as *Capital* in the 1860s, however, there were clear signs of substantial increases in wages in leading capitalist economies, particularly Britain. Marx saw that this historic development could undermine his political project, and struggled for the rest of his life to come to terms with it both theoretically and politically.

Curiously, it is Adam Smith, the earliest of the great classical economists, whose lifetime offered the smallest experience of full-blown industrial capitalism, who would have been least surprised at the emergence of continuous rises in labor productivity and parallel proportional increases in wages. Smith centered his analysis of productivity on the widening division of labor (see Smith, 1937, ch. I and VIII). Although he characteristically evades a sharp confrontation between the increasing returns to the accumulation of labor and capital inherent in the division of labor and the diminishing returns due to limited land resources, Smith seems to have believed that the division of labor could predominate for a long time. Smith's theory of wages is equally delphic, but he does conjure up the comforting vision of rising wages in a progressive capitalist society in which accumulation is steadily increasing population and output.

Modern political economy provides at least one powerful explanation of why industrial capitalist economies achieve systematic increases in labor productivity and stabilize wages as a proportion of national income. If the rates of increase of labor and capital productivity depend on the relative shares of labor and capital in the costs of production, there is a powerful feedback mechanism linking distribution to productivity increases. If the wage share, for example, rises, the rate of increase of labor productivity would also rise, tending to reduce the demand for labor and putting downward pressure on the level of wages. This feedback would act as a kind of social thermostat to stabilize the wage share at the level at which the induced increase in capital productivity is close to zero, which is a necessary condition for a stable relationship between accumulation and growth of the labor force. This theory has remarkable implications. It suggests that the wage share in the long run is completely independent of the forces of capitalist thrift leading to accumulation and of labor force growth, being determined entirely by factors relating to the bias of technical change. In this sense it provides a sharp alternative to the neoclassical vision of distribution reflecting the social scarcities of inputs to production.

While this theory has great explanatory power, it also raises important unresolved questions about the foundations of the theory of induced technical change. The classical distinction between labor, capital, and land inputs to production rests on their quite different conditions of reproduction, that is, in modern terms, on their different mechanisms of supply. The theory of induced technical change, on the other hand, rests on the pressures on individual capitalists to reduce costs in general. The individual capitalist has no reason to distinguish labor, capital, and land inputs to production, since they all appear simply as elements of cost. Why, then, should the rates of increase of productivity of labor and capital respond particularly to their shares in costs? The answer may lie in the *generalizability* of techniques that increase the productivity of any particular form of labor to other forms of labor, since all labor is the productive effort of conscious human beings.

The puzzle of distribution

Wage levels are the outcomes of implicit or explicit bargaining between individual workers and employers. Looking at this process from the worker's subjective point of view it is not hard to understand why the classical economists thought wages would tend to be pushed down to some minimum level. Workers in capitalist societies typically feel insecure, feel that they face vigorous competition from a large number of other equally- or better-qualified workers, and as a result tend often to accept whatever wage is on offer. The wage bargain, as Marx is at pains to point out in his analysis of labor-power as a commodity (Marx, 1976, ch. 6), is not an agreement between the capitalist and worker to share the value added by the worker's labor. The worker surrenders control over her or his capacity to produce for a set period of time in exchange for the wage, regardless of how well the capitalist actually succeeds in turning the capacity to produce into a product and sales revenue. Thus, there is no reason to think that capitalist employers will automatically reward workers for higher productivity with higher wages.

Furthermore, workers form a large and dispersed group that faces major difficulties in controlling the boundary conditions of the labor market. A rising wage easily attracts potential workers from other activities, such as subsistence farming, and from other regions and countries into the labor market, as Marx emphasized in his discussion of reserve armies of labor. While the Malthusian mechanisms of fertility and mortality play a much smaller role in regulating the supply of labor-power to an industrial capitalist society than in sustaining a demographic equilibrium in pre-capitalist societies, the world population explosion that followed the rise of industrial capitalism reminds us of their latent force.

The Classical political economists were hard-headed enough to reject the idea that social solidarity, morality, or good-will would do much to ensure that workers as a class shared in general rises of labor productivity. Even if some individual capitalists were to make a practice of sharing productivity gains with their workers, they would quickly find themselves at a disadvantage with respect to even marginally less generous or responsible competitors.

Thus, Malthus, Ricardo, and Marx looked for some ultimate floor to the wage, with the expectation that wages would normally be forced down to this floor. Malthus wanted to locate this floor in biological terms, in the minimal standard of living required for the successful reproduction of workers as a class. Marx, following Smith, puts more emphasis on the "social and historical" factors mediating the material requirements for the reproduction of workers, without explaining very clearly how these social and historical factors actually work. Smith acknowledges the notion of a minimum subsistence standard of living as a wage regulator, but also seems to believe that wages might be pulled up well above this level indefinitely in an expanding and prosperous capitalist economy.

To what mechanisms, then, can we attribute the actual historical experience in industrial capitalist societies of wages rising roughly at the same rate as labor productivity, so that wage shares have remained roughly constant over long periods of time? Three fundamental mechanisms suggest themselves.

First, there might be a systematic tendency for the subsistence minimum standard of living of workers to rise along with labor productivity, due to rising requirements of training, health, and social skills at higher productivity levels. It is hard to imagine, for example, ragged and intermittently starving workers running sophisticated modern technology. But the experience of "newly industrializing countries" in the last half of the twentieth century shows that the range of worker standards of living compatible with advanced technology is very broad. There is also the question of the degree to which technology has been shaped to workers' styles and conditions of life rather than the reverse.

Second, workers' efforts to organize themselves politically and economically through political parties and unions to control the boundary conditions of the labor market might give them enough leverage over wages to secure a claim on a proportion of productivity gains. The immense political struggles over the right to unionize and its limits in advanced capitalist economies suggest that both capitalists and workers perceive this as a critical social dynamic. But the degree and influence of unionization varies immensely even among the advanced industrial capitalist societies, much more than the wage share or the elasticity of the wage with respect to labor productivity. A sharp increase in the wage share in the course of rapid capital accumulation has been a common experience in many newly industrializing countries with weak or repressed labor rights, such as South Korea.

Third, the forces of capital accumulation might be so strong as to tend constantly to outrun effective supplies of labor-power, thus forcing wages to rise to ration excess demand for labor. This Smithian mechanism is the simplest and most plausible of the explanations, but carries with it subtle and difficult questions of interpretation and ideology. Even advanced industrial capitalist economies tend to operate with a significant margin of unemployed labor, which can balloon up for long periods to large absolute numbers of unemployed. This observation tends to argue against the assumption that full employment or labor scarcity plays the dominant role in mediating wage increases. This explanation tends all too easily to slide into an apology for capitalist social relations in the form of "trickle-down" economics, the argument that strengthening profitability and capital accumulation are the best way to advance the interests of workers as a class.

The three mechanisms are far from mutually exclusive, and in fact tend strongly to reinforce and interact with each other. A tight labor market provides a favorable ground for union formation and bargaining. Unionization tends to professionalize the workforce and create pressures to build higher standards of living into workers' expectations and self-image. On the other hand, a sharp rise in the wage share in income reduces the ability of capitalists to accumulate and sets in motion a process of weakening labor demand and increasing unemployment. In periods of rapid accumulation the third mechanism, labor market scarcity, may play the key role in advancing wages, which get built into historical and social expectations of workers' standards of living. In periods of slumping accumulation, the difficulty capitalists face in renegotiating wage levels with their ongoing employees and the resistance of unions may significantly slow the fall in wages.

Marx, without denying the importance of "over-accumulation" of capital and a consequent rise in wages as one aspect of the capitalist business cycle, argued that over the long period deeper forces regulated the size of the reserve army of labor and the rate of exploitation (the ratio of the profit to the wage share in income) (Marx, 1981, ch. 13). A rise in the wage share, in Marx's analysis, tends to be self-limiting because by reducing profitability it reduces the rate of capital accumulation and hence the growth in the demand for labor. In addition, a rise in the wage share tends to hasten the growth of labor productivity and thus create more technological unemployment, renewing the reserve army of labor. (We will return to this theme below.) The inverse forces tend to correct a fall in the wage share as well over the long period, though Marx tended to put less emphasis on this implication of his analysis for obvious political reasons.

The systematic explanation of wage movements both over the long period and over the business cycle is a key problem for the modern development of

Classical and Marxian political economy. Despite the existence of a lot of research examining this problem in specific historical situations, the political and policy effectiveness of these ideas has been hobbled by the reluctance of the Classical school as a whole to acknowledge the pervasive positive effect of the accumulation of capital and periodic scarcity of labor-power on wages. Putting this mechanism in its appropriate place in a synthetic understanding of wage dynamics is critical to forwarding Classical and Marxian positions.

The Goodwin model

In analytical terms the most elegant expression of these dynamics in the Classical/Marxian literature is Richard Goodwin's model of the capitalist labor market (Goodwin, 1967). Denoting employment by N and the potential labor force by L, Goodwin assumes that the rate of change in the wage per worker, w, will be proportional to the excess of the employment rate $e = N/L$ over an institutionally given level e_0, at which the real wage would not change. Writing $\hat{w} = \dot{w}/w = (1/w)(\mathrm{d}w/\mathrm{d}t)$ for the growth rate of the wage, and δ for the factor of proportionality:

$$\hat{w} = \delta(e - e_0) \tag{2.1}$$

This formulation has several shortcomings. The parameter e_0 can all too easily be interpreted as "full-employment" or a "non-accelerating inflation rate of unemployment," which can become a shibboleth in the formation of macroeconomic demand policy. As it stands this formulation has no explicit treatment of the other two mechanisms influencing wage determination, social expectations and class struggle, though they can be introduced into the analysis in an *ad hoc* way through changes in the parameters. But as a simple stylized representation of long period dynamics, the Goodwin model is at least a promising starting point.

The mechanism of capital accumulation

The Classical political economists and Marx agree in regarding capital accumulation as primarily arising from the reinvestment of profits, on the ground that, while individual worker households save (to provide for retirement, protection against income fluctuations, the education of children, among other motives), their saving is largely offset in any period by the spending of other worker households (e.g. to maintain consumption in retirement or in the face of unemployment).

In order to have a simple representation of the Classical mechanism of accumulation, consider a typical capitalist household. This typical capitalist has wealth J which yields an average return r, and consumes at the rate $c(t)$, in order to maximize the discounted present value of a logarithmic felicity:

$$\max \int_0^\infty \ln c(t) e^{-\beta t} \, dt$$

subject to $\dot{J} = rJ - c$

Here, $\beta > 0$ is a positive discount rate. The capitalist achieves this maximization by setting $c = \beta J$ so that $\dot{J} = (r - \beta)J$, or $\hat{J} = r - \beta$. The parameter β represents the force of capitalist thrift (with higher levels of β corresponding to less thrifty capitalists). If capitalist wealth consists entirely of accumulated capital, K, we have

$$\hat{K} = r - \beta$$

The choice of a logarithmic felicity function has the serendipitous effect of making the capitalist's consumption depend only on the current level of wealth, regardless of the path of rates of return anticipated in the future, and thus to make accumulation depend only on the current rate of return, r, and the thrift parameter, β.

Goodwin combined a similar model of capital accumulation with the labor market model sketched above to provide an elegant explanation of accumulation and fluctuation in the process of capital accumulation. His model rests on the mutual feedback between wages and the profit rate, on the one hand, and the profit rate and the demand for labor-power, on the other. The average profit rate in a capitalist economy, r, is the ratio of profits, the difference between the value of output, X, and wages, W, to the value of accumulated capital, K. If we write $\omega = W/X$ for the wage share, $x = X/N$ for the productivity of labor, and $\rho = X/K$ for the output-capital ratio, the profit rate is:

$$r = \frac{X - W}{K} = \left(1 - \frac{w}{x}\right)\rho = (1 - \omega)\rho$$

Given the productivity of labor, $x = X/N$ and the productivity of capital, $\rho = X/K$, and abstracting from short-run substitutability between labor and capital inputs, employment will be proportional to the capital stock, $N = (\rho/x)K$, and if labor and capital productivity are growing at the rates $\hat{x} \equiv \gamma$ and $\hat{\rho} \equiv \chi$, the rate of growth of employment will be $\hat{N} = \hat{K} + \chi - \gamma$. Then if potential labor grows at the rate n, the employment ratio obeys the relation:

$$\hat{e} = \hat{N} - \hat{L} = r - \beta + \chi - \gamma - n = \left(1 - \frac{w}{x}\right)\rho - \beta + \chi - \gamma - n$$

(2.2)

Given x, ρ, β, n, γ, χ, and e_0, equations (2.1) and (2.2) comprise a two-dimensional dynamical system in (e, w), which, as Goodwin shows, exhibits paths of fluctuating growth.

The steady-state equilibria of this version of the Goodwin model, which exist only if $\chi = \gamma = 0$, so that labor and capital productivity are constant over time, can be calculated by setting $\hat{w} = 0$ and $\hat{e} = 0$, yielding the steady state values $e^* = e_0$, $r^* = (1 - w^*/x)\rho = \beta + n$. Higher labor productivity, x, corresponds to a higher steady-state wage in order to keep the wage share constant. Higher capital productivity, ρ, corresponds to a higher steady-state wage and wage share. An increase in β, representing reduced capitalist thrift, or in n, corresponds to a higher steady-state profit rate, and thus to a lower steady-state wage and wage share. These comparative dynamics results constitute the basic "intuition" of the Classical approach to growth constrained by the growth of potential labor supply.

The puzzle of productivity change

As we have seen, Malthus and Ricardo expected diminishing returns on account of limited land and natural resources to dominate the long-run pattern of productivity growth in capitalist economies. History has not been kind to this point of view, since industrialized capitalist economies tend in fact to exhibit substantial, if fluctuating, rates of growth of labor productivity over long historical periods. This is the pattern foreseen by Marx and Smith. Smith expected the widening division of labor accompanying capital accumulation to outweigh diminishing returns to limited land. Marx argued that the essential genius of capitalist production lay in its bias toward technical progressivity, due to the competitive pressure on individual capitalists to lower costs and their ability to control innovation as the organizers of social production. (Smith's and Marx's ways of describing this process are not inconsistent, though they emphasize different moments.)

Both Smith and Marx foresaw a systematic bias in the pattern of technical change in industrial capitalist economies, in which the productivity of labor (the ratio of measures of real output to the employed labor force) would rise, and the ratio of real output to accumulated real output used as capital (which, in the interests of economy of words we can call the productivity of capital) would fall. Since the profit rate is $r = (1 - \omega)\rho$, a fall in capital productivity holding the wage share constant evidently lowers the profit rate. Both Smith and Marx foresee a tendency for the profit rate to fall with capital accumulation and technical progress in the course of economic development. Marx develops this idea in some detail in his famous and highly controversial discussion of the "tendency for the profit rate to fall" (Marx, 1981, ch. 13). There is evidence that this tendency has operated over some, but not all, historical periods of capitalist economic development (see Duménil and Lévy, 1994; Foley and Michl, 1999).

In fact, what evidence we have strongly suggests that industrial capitalist economies experience rather large continuous increases in labor productivity, on the order of 1–3 percent per year, and much smaller changes in capital productivity, on the order of zero percent per year or slightly negative. As in the case of distribution, it is worth reflecting on how very different the world would be if the actual pattern of technical change were the opposite. If the output–capital ratio were to rise at a rate of 1–3 percent per year for a long time, with stagnant labor productivity, capitalism would rapidly come to an end because the means of production would become so easy to acquire. The tendential rise in capital productivity would tend to push the profit rate up, increasing accumulation and the demand for labor, and raising the wage share toward unity. (Keynes, 1936, sketches this scenario in his account of the "euthanasia of the rentier" as a result of sustained capital accumulation.)

The controversy over Marx's theory of the tendency of the profit rate to fall centers on the question of why technical change in capitalist economies should have a labor-saving, capital-using (or capital-neutral) bias to begin with. While labor-saving, capital-neutral technical change is often called "Harrod-neutral," Foley and Michl (1999) call labor-saving, capital-using technical change "Marx-biased." The neoclassical tradition tends to see technical change in industrial capitalist economies as the reflection of largely autonomous or exogenous advances in science and engineering in economic production. The bedrock of neoclassical economics is the view that market prices reflect social scarcities of limited resources. In this perspective there is no basis for an analytical distinction between labor and capital inputs to production. Both types of input appear to the individual capitalist as elements of cost, and the capitalist has the same incentive to reduce cost, regardless of the abstract categorization of the input (as Samuelson, 1965, and Salter, 1960, argue).

Marx himself acknowledges this basic point, and, in fact, devotes a considerable amount of exposition to it. In Marx's language the capitalist system obliterates the distinction between capital and labor insofar as the individual capitalist sees only a "cost-price" of output comprising both types of inputs (Marx, 1981, ch. 1). In Marx's view labor is the ultimate source of value, so that the individual capitalist is mistaken; reduced capital costs cannot increase the aggregate surplus value of the system as a whole except indirectly through changes in the value of labor-power mediated by the complex operation of the labor market. Thus the problem of explaining the macroeconomic bias in patterns of productivity change recapitulates the deep theoretical controversy over the "labor theory of value" which has divided and vexed political economy over many years (see Foley, 1986).

Innovation, distribution, and the profit rate

In 1964, Charles Kennedy resurrected a suggestion of John Hicks that there might be a link between the macroeconomic bias toward labor-saving technical change and the fact that the wage share in income (or, equivalently costs) tends to be high (Hicks, 1932; Kennedy, 1964). Kennedy proposed that the typical, or representative, capitalist firm might face an "innovation possibilities schedule" showing, for a given investment in innovation, the trade-off between the rate of growth of labor productivity, $\gamma = \hat{x}$, and the rate of growth of capital productivity, $\chi = \hat{\rho}$, expressed as a functional dependence $\gamma = \phi[\chi]$. Kennedy postulated that this trade-off would exhibit diminishing returns in that successive increases in the growth of labor productivity would require larger sacrifices of capital productivity. A capitalist firm seeking to maximize the rate of decrease of its costs will choose the pattern of technical change on this schedule where its slope is equal to the negative of the ratio of the profit share to the wage share. For example, a unit of output requires $1/x$ units of labor input and $1/\rho$ units of capital, so the cost is $(w/x) + (r/\rho) = 1$. Logarithmic differentiation gives the rate of decrease of costs, taking the wage and profit rate as given, as $\omega\gamma + (1 - \omega)\chi$, which will be maximized, given $\gamma = \phi[\chi]$ when $\phi'[\chi] = -(1 - \omega)/\omega$. Given the assumption of diminishing returns to labor-saving innovation, this implies that the rate of increase of labor productivity will be an increasing function of the wage share, and the rate of increase of capital productivity will be an increasing function of the profit share

$$\hat{x} = \gamma[\omega], \qquad \gamma' > 0$$
$$\hat{\rho} = \chi[1 - \omega], \quad \chi' > 0$$

where square brackets [ ] indicate functional arguments.

Duménil and Lévy (1995) reach a similar conclusion concerning the dependence of the average rate of technical change on distribution in a model in which capitalist firms simply select candidate technical innovations that are thrown up by a random process which is symmetric with respect to saving capital and labor on the criterion of reducing costs at current prices (i.e. the current wage). Technical changes which are "viable" in the language of Okishio (1961), lie above a line whose slope is equal to the negative of the ratio of the profit share to the wage share. As a result the mean of the truncated distribution of viable innovations has the rate of change of labor productivity increasing in the wage share.

The Goodwin–Kennedy model: induced technical change

Adding the theory of induced technical change to the Goodwin system makes labor productivity, x, and capital productivity, ρ, endogenous or state variables of the system. It is mathematically convenient to introduce the new variables "effective employment," xN, and "effective potential labor," xL, and the corresponding "effective wage" $\overline{w} = w/x$ to analyze this system. The rate of growth of the effective wage is just $\hat{\overline{w}} = \hat{w} - \hat{x}$. Noting that the effective wage, w/x, is the wage share, ω, the extended Goodwin system can be written in three state variables, ω, e, and ρ and corresponding laws of motion:

$$\hat{\omega} = \delta(e - e_0) - \gamma[\omega], \quad \gamma' > 0 \tag{2.3}$$

$$\hat{e} = (1 - \omega)\rho - \beta + \chi[1 - \omega] - \gamma[\omega] - n \tag{2.4}$$

$$\hat{\rho} = \chi[1 - \omega], \quad \chi' > 0 \tag{2.5}$$

This system can have a steady-state growth path only if $\hat{\rho} = \chi[1 - \omega^*] = 0$, so that capital productivity asymptotically remains constant. But this condition, if it can be met at all, then determines the steady-state wage share independently of all the other parameters in the system, on the basis of the induced technical change mechanism alone. Drandakis and Phelps (1966) and Shah and Desai (1981) reach this conclusion in papers addressed primarily at other issues. (I am indebted to Alexander J. Julius for these references.) Duménil and Lévy have also reached these conclusions in extensions of their model of induced technical change. In particular, this implies that if a stable steady-state exists, the wage share does not depend on the growth of the labor force or capitalist thrift, in contrast to the Classical intuition of the Goodwin model without induced technical change. This determination of the wage share is also at odds with the neoclassical presumption that distribution reflects the relative scarcity inputs to production. In the Classical model neither labor nor capital are essentially scarce in the long run, since capital can be accumulated out of produced output, and labor can be effectively produced through induced technical change. As Duménil and Lévy have suggested, one could interpret the wage share as reflecting the "difficulty" of technical change, as represented by the underlying random production of innovation possibilities in their model, or the position of Kennedy's technical innovation frontier.

Given the steady-state wage share ω^* that satisfies $\chi[1 - \omega^*] = 0$, the steady-state rate of growth of labor productivity will be $\gamma^* = \gamma[\omega^*]$. Then the labor market equation (2.3) determines the steady-state employment rate: $e^* = e_0 + \gamma^*/\delta$. The higher the steady-state rate of growth of labor productivity, the higher must be the employment rate to induce wages per real worker to rise at the same rate as labor productivity.

The remaining steady-state condition, $\hat{e} = 0$, determines the steady-state productivity of capital, $\rho^* = (\beta + n + \gamma^*)/(1 - \omega^*)$. We see now that changes in the rate of growth of potential labor-power, and in capitalist thrift, are absorbed entirely by changes in the productivity of capital, which adapts to make the profit rate just large enough to induce enough capitalist accumulation to balance potential labor force growth. A higher rate of growth of potential labor-power or lower capitalist thrift (a higher β) both increase the steady-state productivity of capital. If a stable economy that had achieved a steady-state growth path were to experience a decline in the growth rate of the supply of labor-power, the wage share would rise transiently, inducing a downward drift in capital productivity to lower the profit rate to compensate.

This induced theory of technical change provides a parsimonious, elegant, and powerful explanation of the observed "stylized facts" of growth in industrial capitalist economies. The mechanism of induced technical change provides a powerful feedback mechanism that stabilizes the wage share, and simultaneously drives the system to low or zero rates of growth of capital productivity. When the rate of growth of capital productivity is zero, however, there are still abundant incentives to labor-saving technical change, so that the bias of technical change toward labor is understandable. The whole process is driven by the fact that initially profitability is so high that capital accumulation constantly threatens to outrun the growth of potential labor-power. The resulting secular upward pressure on wages, operating in a highly uneven and cyclical fashion, gradually reduces profitability and induces steady rates of growth of labor productivity.

Elegant and parsimonious though it may be, there are important objections that could be raised against this vision of capitalist economic development. While there are undoubtedly upward pressures on the wages of the employed, capitalist economies tend to operate with and reproduce astonishingly large labor surpluses in the form of unemployment and developmental backwardness. These labor surpluses can be explained in the model through appropriate choice of the parameters δ, and e_0, but as I remarked above, Goodwin's model of the labor market is at best a first approximation to a much more complex and nuanced analysis. As in all economic models, the attempt to explain immediately observable patterns in terms of deeper structures (in this case the mechanisms of induced technical change) raise inevitable questions about the determination and stability of those deeper structures themselves.

Stability

The relevance of the steady-state growth paths arising from the extended Goodwin–Kennedy system depend on the likelihood that these steady states would be stable. The Jacobian of the system of equations (2.3)–(2.5) is:

$$\begin{pmatrix} -\gamma'\omega^* & \delta\omega^* & 0 \\ (-\rho^* - \chi' - \gamma')e^* & 0 & e^*(1 - \omega^*) \\ -\rho^*\chi' & 0 & 0 \end{pmatrix}$$

The trace is $-\gamma'\omega^* < 0$, the second principal minor is $\delta\omega^*(\rho^* + \chi' + \gamma')e^* > 0$, and the determinant is $-e^*(1 - \omega^*)\chi'\rho^*\delta\omega^* < 0$, under the assumptions of the endogenous technical change model. The system is always stable, but may have a pair of conjugate complex eigenvalues, corresponding to the damped Goodwin predator–prey cycle.

The stability of the system arises from the strong negative feedback through the induced technical change mechanism of the wage share on itself. A rise in the wage share above its steady-state equilibrium level tends to raise the rate of labor-saving technical progress, and lower the profit rate and the rate of capital accumulation. These factors both tend to reduce the growth of the demand for labor-power and reduce the wage and the wage share. A shock to the wage share may set off a transient Goodwin cycle through the labor market-accumulation interaction as well. If the basic hypothesis linking the wage share strongly to the rates of labor- and capital-saving technical change is correct, the tendency for the economy to stabilize around a steady state will be robust.

Foundations of induced technical change theory

The power of the hypothesis linking distributive shares to the macroeconomic bias in technical change to explain pervasive features of industrial capitalist growth constitutes an a priori case for at least being interested in whether it might be true. As I remarked above, the "micro-foundations" of the induced technical change hypothesis are not well understood.

The basic problem is to explain why it makes sense to aggregate what are, concretely, qualitatively different labor and capital inputs into the broad categories of "labor" and "capital." For example, if we had just two types of labor, "skilled" and "unskilled" labor, and two types of capital "heavy machinery" and "light machinery," we would in principle have four shares in costs. Suppose the rate of change of productivity of each of these inputs were dependent on its (and the other inputs') share. The induced technical change hypothesis at the aggregate level of "labor" and "capital" inputs faces all of the contradictions identified in the Cambridge capital controversy (see Harcourt, 1972; Kurz and Salvadori, 1995; Kurz, 2000) over the impossibility of defining coherent composite inputs such as "capital" on the basis of disparate concrete inputs such as different capital goods. Effectively "skilled" and "unskilled" labor (and "heavy" and "light" machinery) would have to be perfect substitutes in production at some technical rate of substitution in order for the aggregate relation between wage and profit shares and rates of increase of labor and capital productivity to hold. The aggregate relation would not work if we aggregated to two inputs, one of which was a composite of skilled labor and heavy machinery, and the other a composite of unskilled labor and light machinery.

From the neoclassical point of view, as I remarked above, there is no rationale for aggregating inputs into categories such as "labor" and "capital." Each type of labor and each capital good represents a different scarce resource for neoclassical theory. Whatever incentives there are for capitalist firms to economize on one of these inputs are exactly the same as the incentives to economize on any other. In the absence of some concrete engineering or technical constraints (which will be constantly changing over the development of capitalism), there is no reason to predict that any one aggregate of these disparate inputs will experience technical change at any different rate from any other aggregate. This leads Samuelson (1965) to the hypothesis that in the absence of other information, we should expect the same rate of productivity increase for any input. If capitalist firms put the same effort into reducing each dollar of their costs, then we would expect each component of cost to decline at roughly the same rate, and since the quantities of each input are weighted in cost by the input price, this would imply that all of the productivities should rise at the same rate. But then there would be no dependence of the rate of increase of productivity of labor and capital aggregates on their shares at the macroeconomic level. This is a tempting theoretical argument, but appears to be completely wrong empirically, given the strong macroeconomic evidence for the patterns of Harrod-neutral or Marx-biased technical progress in the data.

The neoclassical point of view has a similar problem explaining the historical constancy of the wage share. (Solow's, 1958, attempt to debunk the claim of a constant wage share addresses the question of the magnitude of fluctuations of the wage share over time rather than the question, raised here, of the historical constancy of the wage share in the face of dramatic secular increases in labor productivity.) If "labor" and "capital" are essentially arbitrary collections of inputs that are subject to random, patternless rates of increase of technical productivity, we would expect the resulting measured shares to drift randomly, in contradiction to the data we observe. These considerations have driven the neoclassical growth literature to sweep the issues of distribution and technical change under the rug of the Cobb–Douglas specification of the production function, in which the wage share becomes an exogenous parameter, and the measurement of the pattern of technical change is completely confounded by the substitutability of labor and capital inputs, so that it is possible without fear of empirical contradiction simply to assume a Harrod-neutral pattern to technical change.

The Classical political economists, in contrast, did have a compelling rationale for treating capital and labor (and land) inputs as analytically unified categories. They distinguished each of these broad categories of inputs by its conditions of reproduction. Capital inputs were produced as commodities within the capitalist system of production, typically with constant or declining costs of production with scale. Land inputs were gifts of nature that were unreproducible at any cost. Labor inputs were human beings, reproduced not directly as commodities by capitalist relations of production, but by deeper and more complex human social forces. Thus the conditions of reproduction, or supply, of labor, capital, and land inputs provide a coherent analytical base for distinguishing them. (Marginalist and neoclassical theory is based on the assumption that it makes sense, at least in the short run, to regard capital and labor inputs as fixed in supply, just like Classical land, and thus to analyze profits and wages as forms of rent.)

Unfortunately, this analytical distinction does not immediately provide a foundation for the theory of induced technical change, which is a theory of changes in the demand for inputs, not of their conditions of supply. If we regard the basic locus of the process of induced technical change as the efforts of the capitalist firm to reduce its cost, we face the problem that the capitalist market makes labor-power, capital goods, and land resources appear to the individual capitalist as qualitatively indistinguishable elements of cost, all available on the market for a price. Marx makes this a major theme of his theoretical exposition (Marx, 1976, ch. 8). Marx argues that the source of all value is the expenditure of labor, and thus that there is a real and vital distinction between what he calls "constant," or non-expanding capital, the value of means of production purchased by the capitalist, which reappears on average unchanged in the value of the product and "variable," or expanding capital, the value of wages expended to purchase labor-power, which appears expanded on average in the value of the product by the addition of the surplus value arising from the unpaid labor time capitalists extract from the labor-power of workers (Foley, 1986, ch. 3). The distinction between constant capital ("dead" labor, in Marx's colorful jargon) and variable capital ("living" labor) is essential to Marx's analysis of exploitation, the historical role of capitalism, capitalist crisis, and the long-run tendencies of capitalist accumulation (as it is less explicitly for Ricardo and Smith as well). But Marx explains very carefully that the market relations of capitalism make this fundamental distinction invisible to the participants in the process, particularly capitalist entrepreneurs. (Marx saw the hallmark of what he called "vulgar" political economy as a refusal to recognize the distinction between constant and variable capital, and to analyze the economy at the level of "appearance" in which all inputs to production, produced means of production and labor-power, are treated as qualitatively equivalent.) But if the operation of the market for inputs to production and competition effectively obscure the distinction between labor and capital inputs for capitalist entrepreneurs, how can we explain the dependence of induced rates of technical change in labor and capital inputs on their shares in costs?

The two theories I have already mentioned, Kennedy's assumption of an "innovation possibilities frontier" and Duménil and Lévy's evolutionary model of technical change, effectively assume that the conditions of technical change for capital and labor inputs are different and rival as a primitive of the theory. Kennedy does this by drawing the innovation possibilities frontier as convex in the space of rates of increase of capital and labor productivity to begin with. Duménil and Lévy accomplish the same analytical end by assuming that the distribution of randomly produced innovative technologies is symmetric with respect to the interchange of rates of increase of labor and capital productivity. In each case the assumption justifying the treatment of rates of increase of productivity in terms of labor and capital aggregates is built into the structure of the mathematical specification of the model.

From a common-sense perspective, however, there is a strong reason to expect self-organization in the patterns of labor-saving and capital-saving technical change in a capitalist society. Labor in all its forms is the effort of conscious human beings, so that we would not be surprised to find that labor-saving innovations were relatively easy to generalize from one type of labor to another. Thus if, as Samuelson believes, capitalists put an equal effort of cost reduction into each dollar of costs, but the discovery of a way to save a dollar of wage costs in one aspect of production suggests similar methods in other aspects of production, the total effort to reduce labor costs would be proportional to the wage share. This line of argument suggests that there could be a strong statistical correlation between the wage share and increases in labor productivity, even if particular labor-saving discoveries are specific to particular phases of capitalist production.

The labor theory of value

The theory of induced technical change and the problem of the bias in patterns of technical change in the course of capitalist economic development do not immediately evoke the controversies that swirl around the "labor theory of value," but there is a close connection between these issues nonetheless. The labor theory of value is most often presented as an approach to the problem of the determination of relative prices in a competitive capitalist economy. In its simplest incarnation, the labor theory of value proposes to explain relative prices of commodities as reflecting the relative amounts of labor time (somehow aggregated out of the various concrete laboring activities that go into the production process) directly and indirectly expended in their production. The equalization of profit rates through competition among capitals may require a reallocation of this labor time among different sectors through an adjustment of relative prices. Marx's controversial discussion of the "transformation problem" (Marx, 1981, ch. 9) is centered on the claim that this reallocation of labor time can be conceptualized in such a way that the total money value realized in sales is proportional to the total labor time embodied in the commodities, and the surplus value represented by profits is proportional to the unpaid living labor time. The technical difficulties involved in proving these identities in various models of capitalist production have generated a large literature on the transformation problem, embodying a vigorous and sometimes repetitive controversy that shows no signs of exhausting its participants (Foley, 1986, 2000a).

But we see from the discussion of the theory of induced technical change that there are other quite fundamental issues connected with the labor theory of value at the macroeconomic level that have little to do with the determination of relative prices. The deepest of these is the question of whether or not there is any significant analytical difference between labor and produced means of production as inputs to production. This difference seemed self-evident to the Classical political economists and Marx, all of whom base their discussions of capitalist production on the idea that labor, capital, and land are distinct inputs to production, even though capitalist social relations makes them all appear as indistinguishable priced commodities on the market. In this perspective the explanation of wages, profit, and rent require different theories adapted to the different conditions of reproduction of labor, means of production, and land. On the other hand, marginalist economics and the neoclassical point of view that grew out of it start from the abstraction that all inputs to production can be regarded symmetrically as scarce resources commanding rents, and thus that wages, profits, and rent can be explained by a single unified theory of factor pricing. Some followers of the Classical point of view have reached a similar theoretical conclusion by a different route. For example, both Sraffa and von Neumann sometimes represent labor as a commodity reproduced effectively by the same processes as other means of production, and thus priced according to the same principles. (For these Classically-inspired economists the unifying principle is the equalization of profit rates, not scarcity rents.) One way to interpret the broad category of labor theories of value is to regard them as starting from the insight that labor has to be treated distinctly from land and produced means of production in analyzing capitalist economies.

The controversy over the theory of induced technical change recapitulates this fundamental division in economic theory, and thus resurrects these old, unresolved theoretical questions. As we have seen, the theory only makes sense if we decide for some reason or other to regard labor and capital inputs as natural categories for the explanation of technical change. It is not surprising that this starting point leads to a theory of distribution which is sharply at odds with the neoclassical idea that factor prices represent relative scarcities of resources. It is perhaps somewhat more surprising that it leads to a theory of distribution equally at odds with the modern Classical idea that input prices represent real costs of reproduction.

A way out of the capital theory dilemma?

One of the great contributions of the Classical political economic tradition to twentieth century economics was the "Cambridge capital controversy," the debates between Classical and neoclassical theorists over the concept of an aggregate capital stock (see Burmeister, 2000). This controversy has some striking parallels to the issues that arise in the literature on induced technical change. From the point of view of an individual capitalist firm, which takes input prices as independent of its own decisions as to input mix, it is possible to aggregate any subset of inputs consistently. The firm can be regarded as making its input decision at a very concrete level, at which it distinguishes many types and grades of labor input and many specific means of production, each with its own price, and striving to minimize cost over all of its technically and socially feasible production plans. Or, we can equally consistently regard the firm as aggregating all of the labor inputs into one wage budget, and all of the means of production into one capital budget, and considering the cost consequences of altering the proportions of its spending at this level. Since the firm takes input prices of both labor and intermediate inputs as independent of its decision, input prices are a natural aggregator of costs.

In fact, the firm could be regarded equally consistently as aggregating some categories of labor and intermediate goods together in one broad input and other categories of labor and intermediate goods together in another broad input, and studying the problem of cost minimization at this level.

The early neoclassical political economists fell into a "fallacy of composition" by assuming that because it was possible to regard capital and labor inputs consistently at the firm level, it was equally legitimate to regard them as input aggregates at the macroeconomic level. The fallacy arises because input prices can be consistently regarded as independent of input mix decisions for the individual firm, but input prices clearly depend on aggregate input mix decisions in the aggregate. The original motivation for this line of thinking in the work of economists such as John Bates Clark appears to have been the desire to represent profit incomes as arising symmetrically with labor incomes as reflections of the relative scarcity of inputs, and thus to legitimize profit incomes ideologically. Later the same fallacy led to the practice of representing aggregate value added as functionally related to aggregate labor and capital inputs through a "production function" in growth models. In retrospect one might wonder why the neoclassical political economists felt it necessary to introduce capital and labor aggregates into their theory at all, since those concepts have no analytical foundations in the neoclassical worldview.

The aim of the Cambridge capital controversy was to expose the analytical fallacy involved in regarding the aggregate value of capital as a distribution-independent measure of intermediate inputs to production. In making this argument the English Cantabrigians, among whom Italian economists played a central role, representing the Classical political economy tradition, centered the debate on the case of a capitalist economy with fixed technology facing variations in distribution in the form of changes in the wage or profit rate. The fact that in general models there is, for a variety of mathematical reasons, no monotonic relationship between the aggregate value of intermediate capital inputs to production and the profit rate exploded the claim that aggregate production functions could be rigorously used to represent complex multi-input production systems. (While the American Cantabrigians representing the neoclassical tradition were forced to accept the validity of these claims, they and their successors unrepentantly continued to develop growth theory based on aggregate production functions.)

The Classical victory in this debate now appears to have a Pyrrhic aspect. The problem is that the distinction between capital and labor inputs at a macroeconomic level is natural to the Classical political economic point of view. It is in fact Classical political economy, not neoclassical marginalism, that has strong arguments for regarding labor and capital as valid abstractions for a capitalist economy. The methods of the Classical political economists and Marx put the aggregate value of capital at the very center of the analysis of capital accumulation and the evolution of capitalist economies. It is the accumulation of capital value that drives the growth of population and output in the Classical tradition, and thus indirectly through the division of labor, raises the productivity of labor. In delegitimating the aggregate value of capital, the Cambridge controversy has tended to cut the modern descendants of the Classical political economy tradition off from one of its vital conceptual roots.

The perspective of induced technical change may offer a way out of this impasse. The paradigm of induced technical change suggests a different analytical problem for the Classical tradition. Instead of analyzing a capitalist economy with fixed technology facing varying distributional conditions, the induced technical change paradigm suggests studying a capitalist economy which is constantly adapting its technology to relatively stable conditions of distribution. The simple, highly aggregated, models we have at this point suggest that in this setting the value of capital may be regulated, not by the equalization of profit rates given technology, but by systematic changes in technology. This does not lead back to the illegitimate neoclassical claim that the value of capital represents a real scarce input to production independent of distribution, nor, as we have seen, to the conflation of wages and profits as different manifestations of a unified process of imputation of rents to scarce resources. In the induced technical change model the value of capital is important socially because it represents the wealth of the capitalists, and regulates their consumption and accumulation behavior, which in turn influences the demand for labor-power and the conditions of the labor market. There is a logic, according to the induced technical change theory, regulating the ratio of the value of output to the value of capital, and hence the "capital-intensity" of production, but it is a logic of dynamic feedback through the accumulation process, not a logic of static allocational scarcity.

Self-organization in economic history

The theory of induced bias in technical change is a striking example of the way in which self-organizing tendencies of complex systems can manifest themselves in concrete historical developments. The theory explains observed regularities in capitalist economies (the Harrod-neutrality or Marx-bias of technical change and the self-regulation of the wage share) without claiming to explain the specific path of technical innovation, or the particular types of new methods of production that emerge along that path.

The structure of this explanation is worth careful study. It is because capitalist economic institutions put the control of technical innovation in the hands of a class, the capitalists, who have both the means and the compulsion to pursue productivity increases in the guise of cost-reduction. The fact that technical change presents itself to capitalists as a problem of cost-reduction has far-reaching consequences for the paths of technical change that actually emerge. The fact that the dynamics of technical innovation are embedded in specifically capitalist economic structures strongly conditions the patterns the system displays.

This particular example is all the more valuable because there are very few cases where we can observe self-organizing patterns over such long time intervals. The evolution of labor and capital productivity under capitalist social relations of production is thus a kind of model of what we might expect over long periods of time in similar situations involving cost incentives to innovation. One problem to which this method can be applied is the question of the impact of efforts to control the environmental impact of production through cost incentives, which is the theme of Chapter 3.

3 Can political economy save us from global warming?

With the emergence of industrial capitalism, human productive activity has achieved a scale that has important impacts on the world ecological and environmental systems. The management of this impact is one of the fundamental challenges facing us over the coming centuries. Industrial capitalism and the accompanying explosion of the world human population have effects on a host of environmental systems, including fresh water cycles, biodiversity, the ozone layer, and desertification. I will concentrate here on one of the most prominent of these problems, global warming, to look at what political economic analysis has to say about the management of these issues.

Scientific concern about global warming arises from the observation that industrial capitalism has found most of the energy it uses in the burning of fossil fuels, particularly petroleum and coal. When these fuels are burned they release not only the energy stored in them through ancient photosynthesis, but also significant amounts of carbon dioxide and methane. These gases, when released into the atmosphere, tend to prevent the radiation of energy from the earth to space, and as a result raise the earth's surface temperature through the "greenhouse effect." A significant rise in the earth's temperature can have many complicated effects on climate, including increased severity of storms, higher sea levels which may inundate coastal regions inhabited at present by a large proportion of the earth's population, and higher agricultural yields at high latitudes.

While scientific controversy over the exact magnitude and timing of these effects continues to be vigorous, there is persuasive evidence that they are real and potentially of a magnitude to be a legitimate focus of public concern and policy intervention. A survey of the current state of scientific debate on this problem can be found in Intergovernmental Panel on Climate Change, Working Group II, 2001.

Global warming has two fundamental political economic aspects. First, although all parts of the earth will experience the impact of global warming, different parts of the planet will experience very different costs and benefits from efforts to control greenhouse gas emissions. Second, the geophysical scenario of global warming unfolds over a very long time scale compared to other political economic phenomena. The global warming scenario unfolds on a time scale of two hundred to four hundred years, due to the geophysical time constants (such as the half-life of atmospheric carbon dioxide) involved. This greatly exceeds the longest time scales considered in most economic models, which range from business cycle model horizons of 2–5 years, through investment planning model horizons of 5–25 years, long-run growth model horizons of 10–50 years, to demographic models with horizons of 25–100 years. The basic problems of global warming concern the management of the geographical and generational distribution of costs and benefits of various methods of controlling greenhouse gas emission. A more comprehensive discussion of these issues can be found in Cline (1997).

I will begin by looking at what neoclassical economics has to offer as a perspective on this problem, and then turn to the potential insights we might gain from a classical political economic approach.

The welfare economics of global warming

Neoclassical economic analysis of the global warming problem begins by regarding global environmental quality, including world climate, as an unappropriated and therefore underpriced "public good." (I would like to thank Graciela Chichilnisky and Geoffrey Heal for extensive discussions on these issues.) Every nation and its individual productive enterprises and households contribute to global warming by burning fossil fuels, but no one pays any direct cost associated with this impact on the environment. As a result the market gives no signal to enterprises and households to adjust either the quantity of output nor technology to control greenhouse gas emissions. As a result we burn in some sense "too much" fossil fuel.

As neoclassical welfare economics sees matters, corrective intervention to control greenhouse gas emissions in the form of direct controls, taxes, or a system of marketable emission permits will yield an economic *surplus* to the global economy. This surplus could be realized as an improvement in the global standard of living either through improved environmental quality or increases in material consumption. If the burning of fossil fuels does indeed impose an externality on the world economy, neoclassical welfare economics argues that there must be a "Pareto-improving" strategy that increases the standard of living of all regions and generations involved. This is a startling claim, since the debate over global warming has been largely framed in terms of the problem of distributing economic *costs* across regions and across generations.

Let us look at this neoclassical argument a bit more closely. The idea is that on a path of uncontrolled greenhouse gas emissions, the world economy sees too low a price for material consumption, and thus produces and consumes too much. On this path we wind up with a lower standard of living because global environmental quality deteriorates, and we experience direct costs of more severe weather, flooding of coastal areas and the like. Global warming also disrupts productive activities and raises the overall costs of producing material goods in terms of human effort. Thus, the world's population winds up working harder and enjoying life less than would be the case if we adopted policies to limit greenhouse gas emissions.

The regional distribution of costs and benefits

How would this work in practice? Neoclassical welfare economics measures the standard of living ultimately in terms of the consumption of households, including ideally the consumption of intangibles such as environmental quality, not by the volume of their production. How could currently under-developed areas of the world achieve higher paths of average consumption if they are forced to install energy and transportation infrastructures that are more costly as a result of greenhouse gas emissions control?

The key to understanding the economics of this issue is to recognize that underdevelopment is a tremendous advantage in relation to a problem like global warming. The developed industrial capitalist economies are stuck with costly, long-lived energy and transportation investments that depend on high greenhouse gas emissions. Newly developing economies, on the other hand, are just in the process of designing and installing these systems. It is much cheaper to achieve any given level of greenhouse gas emission control through designing and building new energy and transportation systems than it is through retrofitting existing technology. Thus the developing economies are the cheapest place to achieve substantial mitigation in the medium run of fifty to one hundred years. Since the benefits of installing cleaner energy and transport systems in developing economies accrue to the whole world, it should be possible to compensate the developing economies for choosing cleaner technologies through cross-payments from developed economies. In fact, in theory it ought to be possible to *overcompensate*, in the sense that the benefits to the whole world from investments in cleaner energy and transport systems in rapidly growing economies are larger than the costs of those investments. (If this were not the case, there would be no economic rationale for controlling greenhouse gas emissions in the first place.)

One puzzle in the unfolding diplomatic politics of global warming has been the reluctance of rapidly developing economies such as China and India to support measures to control greenhouse gas emissions. This reluctance must be based on their concern that they will not be adequately compensated for their investments in cleaner energy and transport technologies. The problem, from a neoclassical perspective, is how to create an export market for cleaner technologies through which the rapidly developing economies can realize these gains just as surely as they can realize gains from trade in tangible commodities.

But how can the developed countries pay for cleaner technologies in rapidly growing economies without experiencing a fall in the paths of their own standards of living?

The generational distribution of costs and benefits

The benefits of controlling greenhouse gas emissions over the next 100 years will accrue mainly to human generations that will live over the next 300 years, while the costs fall primarily on currently living generations and their immediate successors. From a welfare economics point of view, policy should somehow shift the costs to the future generations who will accrue the benefits. This makes sense when we consider two features of the situation. First, if the historical patterns of industrial capitalist development continue, future generations will be much more productive and therefore richer on average than current generations, and therefore better able to bear the costs of controlling global warming. Second, it is reasonable to suppose that future generations will have a wider range of technological options available to manage their own greenhouse gas emissions problems more cheaply than we can at present.

How can we shift costs of greenhouse gas control to the distant future? Basically, by investing less in tangible economic assets, and thus reducing the economic legacy we leave to the future. In other words we should arrange to maintain, or even increase, our standard of living at the expense of our tangible investment. Future generations will be somewhat worse off than otherwise because they will inherit a somewhat smaller productive capacity, but they will also inherit a higher level of global environmental quality, and in particular a lower concentration of atmospheric greenhouse gases, which they will view as more than compensating them. (Again, if the benefits to them of lower greenhouse gas concentrations did not outweigh the costs in terms of tangible productive facilities, there is no economic case for greenhouse gas abatement to begin with.) The financial counterpart of this real transfer is the financing of investment in greenhouse gas abatement technologies through borrowing, which will crowd out investment in dirtier conventional productive technologies.

Tradable emission permits

Thus the broad outlines of the Pareto-improving deal suggested by the analysis of global warming as an economic externality comprise payments from the developed countries to the developing countries to compensate them for the extra costs of installing cleaner energy and transport technologies, and the financing of these investments and the gradual re-fitting of developed countries' transport and energy systems through borrowing.

One elegant mechanism that achieves these ends is the creation of a global system of tradable emission permits for greenhouse gases (see Carraro, 2000; Chichilnisky and Heal, 2000). If it were possible to enforce this system, it would require any emissions source to acquire a right to emit. The total volume of permits would have to be limited so as to achieve a desirable level of mitigation of global warming. (It might not be easy to determine exactly what this level should be, of course.) Since the permits would be limited, they would be scarce, and would command a price, or royalty. From the point of view of emitters, this would mean that emission of greenhouse gases would become a visible element of economic costs of production and consumption. From the point of view of the owners of the permits, the royalties would constitute an income flow available to finance investment and consumption. It is, in principle, possible to distribute permits initially so as to achieve the flow of resources from the developed to the developing countries required by the broad strategy.

Since permits would generate an income flow in the form of royalties, they could also be capitalized and traded like other financial instruments on financial markets. In this form, they would be a natural collateral against loans, thereby facilitating the financing of emissions control investments through borrowing to shift the real costs of emissions control to the future generations who will presumably be the main beneficiaries.

Political economic realism and welfare economics

There is surely something to be said for this analysis of the global warming problem and its solution. But there are questions as to how relevant many people find these abstract considerations.

Many voices that raise concerns about global warming view it as a kind of retribution for the materialist sins of capitalist economic development. In this view industrial capitalism was a bad idea to begin with, offering only illusory promises of a better life, but actually making human fate worse by destroying our environmental and ecological heritage and enticing humanity into growing to unsustainable population levels. The idea that we can cope with the global warming challenge and *raise* current material consumption levels is unappealing to adherents of this view. Those who have this gloomy view of economic development would question whether future generations will be better off than we, and therefore better able to pay for mitigation of global warming, and thus one of the main premises of the welfare economics analysis. In this view, there is no Pareto-improving way out of the global warming crisis. The problem is that current generations are consuming at an unsustainable rate, and impoverishing future generations. To protect the future, we must accept a sharp decline in our material standard of living, and our levels of production.

Others may doubt that world political processes as presently constituted can reach a Pareto-improving resolution of a major problem like global warming. They see existing power structures as heavily skewed toward the already wealthy developed economies and biased toward present consumption. In this perspective the attempt to institute a system of global greenhouse gas emissions control may simply provide yet another opportunity for the developed capitalist economies to reinforce their global predominance and deny the developing economies the opportunity to catch up economically. Fears and suspicions of this kind clearly are important in the current negotiations, and threaten to derail progress toward a global agreement on these issues.

Finally, many people may question whether material levels of consumption, even including intangibles such as environmental quality, do in fact, or even ought to, play the important role attributed to them by neoclassical welfare analysis. Human beings are motivated as much by spiritual as by material concerns, and perhaps impoverish themselves when they sacrifice the spiritual to the material. From this perspective neoclassical welfare economics' attempt to encompass the problem of global environmental degradation in an extended set of economic accounting methods is a feeble and unconvincing response to a profound existential challenge to our humanity, centering on the issue of our responsibility to the earth and the environment. The welfare economics perspective is still a greedy, human-centered way of looking at the world, which regards the earth and the environment as an instrument to the achievement of human needs and goals. But the earth and the environment are bigger and older than humanity, and have a sacred character that transcends human consumption and welfare, which we must address as well. The urge for an apocalyptic moment in human history is obviously not very well-addressed by the rosy financial visions of a global emission permits scheme.

Dynamic and static substitution

The surplus the world might expect to be able to gain from correcting the greenhouse gas externality depends on what the tradeoffs between production of conventional goods and services and global environmental quality actually are. Neoclassical welfare economics traditionally treats this problem in static terms. The economy is envisioned as facing a menu of technological choices which establish the feasible tradeoffs between the use of different inputs and between inputs and outputs. In the case of the global warming problem, the key tradeoff is how much material consumption we have to give up in order to achieve a particular target for greenhouse gas emissions.

At any given historical period there is a certain latitude in the choice of technology that permits enterprises to make adjustments in their input proportions. If a greenhouse gas emissions permit system were put in place, enterprises would have to pay royalties to emit, and these royalties would constitute a new element in their direct costs of production. This would presumably induce existing enterprises to adjust their technologies so as to reduce greenhouse gas emissions, and create incentives for designers of new power plants and transport systems to build them around cleaner technologies. Inevitably, however, the technologies available at any moment are limited.

As we have seen in the previous chapters, however, industrial capitalism is a powerful mechanism for the generation of new technologies, and there is some reason to believe that the path of technological change is responsive to costs. Considering the very long period of several centuries over which the global warming scenario unfolds, it seems likely that the discovery of new energy technologies will be much more important than substitution using existing technologies. Thus, the model of induced technological change I discussed in Chapter 2 may shed some light on the dynamic tradeoffs the world faces over the global warming scenario.

Accumulation with a land constraint

From the point of view of political economy, the global environment can be regarded as an input into production, parallel with labor and capital goods. The more conventional material output we produce, the more energy we use in doing so, and the more greenhouse gases we emit.

The global warming constraint is in fact exactly parallel to the classical political economists' conception of land as an input to production. The earth's atmosphere and oceans have a certain limited capacity to absorb greenhouse gases without setting off global warming. Once this capacity has been reached, we are powerless to expand it. The classical political economists regarded land resources in the same light. They saw the earth as having a certain endowment of land which human beings could not alter. The appropriation of land as private property, however, would lead to the emergence of rent as a guide to the allocation of scarce land resources. We can adopt classical land and as model for the global environment as an input to production. In what follows I will often refer to the global environment as "land" for brevity.

The absolute carrying capacity of the environment for greenhouse gases is given scientifically, and it is hard to imagine new technologies that would change it very much, short of science fiction scenarios. But the productivity of the environment in terms of material production is subject to the same type of technological innovation that affects labor and capital inputs.

New technologies can reduce the amount of greenhouse gas emission per unit of material output, and in this way increase the effective economic carrying capacity of the earth's environment.

Production

In order to introduce these ideas into the classical model of Chapter 2, we need to represent the negative effect of limited environmental resources on material production (broadly considered to include intangible environmental quality). If we take $Z = \min[xN, \rho K] = xN = \rho K$ to be a "dose" of labor and capital, or "labor-capital," an index of productive effort, then actual output depends both on Z and on the global environment, or land, represented by the variable u:

$$X = G[Z, u]$$

It is convenient to take the function G as a conventional concave, constant-returns-to-scale technology, with positive marginal products for both Z and u.

Given the assumption of constant returns to scale, we can represent output as:

$$X = ug[z] \equiv uG[Z/u, 1]$$

where z is labor-capital per unit of land and $g[z]$ is output per unit of land. While land (or the global environment) is, strictly speaking, given and immutable, the coefficient u can be regarded as representing the technological *effectiveness* of land as an input. An increase in u reflects technological change that reduces the stress of production on the environment, and thus effectively increases the environment or land input. We also assume that the "elasticity of substitution" between land and labor-capital in output is bounded below unity. The g function represents the idea that the impact of the environment on production grows gradually with production. At low levels of production, the environmental constraint hardly matters, but becomes increasingly important as the absolute level of production rises.

Rent and profit

If land is appropriated (or, equivalently, an emissions permit system is in place), competition among enterprises for permits will drive rent (the royalty) in terms of output, v, to equal the marginal product of land, $u(g[z] - zg'[z])$. Given the assumption of constant returns to scale to the G function, the return to the labor-capital dose represented by Z will be its marginal product, $g'[z]$. The labor-capital share in output will be equal to the elasticity of output with respect to labor-capital, $\zeta[z] = zg'[z]$, and the land share of output will be equal to $1 - \zeta[z]$.

Profit is the residual output after rents to land and wages have been deducted. When the output wage is w the wage bill is $wN = wZ/x = uzw/x$. When land is appropriated, total profit is equal to the marginal product of labor-capital less the wage bill, $uz(g'[z] - w/x)$. The rate of profit is total profit divided by the capital stock, $K = Z/\rho = uz/\rho$, so the profit rate is:

$$r = \rho \left(g'[z] - \frac{w}{x} \right)$$

Suppose, on the other hand, that there is no emissions permit system, or, equivalently, that land is not appropriated. In this case there will be no rent (or royalty). Capitalist entrepreneurs will appropriate the whole output once wages are paid as profits. In this case total profit will be $ug[z] - uzw/x$ and the profit rate is:

$$r^* = \rho \left(\frac{g[z]}{z} - \frac{w}{x} \right)$$

Here, $\bar{g}[z] = g[z]/z$ is the *average* product of labor-capital. Thus, the economic impact of pricing the scarce resource, in this case land, or the carrying capacity of the atmosphere, depends on whether capitalist entrepreneurs see the marginal or average product of labor-capital in their calculations of the profit rate.

Accumulation

The emissions permit scheme has an important impact on wealth. The permits themselves, since they yield a stream of revenue in the form of royalties, will be capitalized as wealth. Assuming for simplicity that emission permits are capitalized at a discount rate equal to the profit rate (the rate of return to land when the capitalist has perfect foresight about the path of the land price should be $r = (v/P) + (dP/dt)(1/P)$; to avoid the complications in the dynamic analysis of the model raised by the explicit treatment of perfectly foreseen changes in the price of land we assume stationary expectations, so that $P = v/r$; and the resulting model has the same steady states as the perfect-foresight model) the total value of emission permits, P, will be:

$$P = \frac{v}{r} = \frac{u(g[z] - zg'[z])}{\rho(g'[z] - w/x)}$$

$$= K \frac{g[z]/z - g'[z]}{g'[z] - w/x}$$

$$= K \frac{1 - \zeta[z]}{\zeta[z] - \omega[w, z]}$$

where $\omega[w, z] = (w/x)(z/g[z])$ is the wage share in output.

The representative capitalist has to hold both capital and emission permits in her portfolio. Her total wealth including the emission permits will be $J = K + P = \theta K$, where

$$\theta[w, z] = 1 + \frac{1 - \zeta[z]}{\zeta[z] - \omega[w, z]} = \frac{1 - \omega[w, z]}{\zeta[z] - \omega[w, z]}$$

is the ratio of the value of capital to the value of wealth. Since permits and capital have the same rate of return, r, the capitalist's wealth grows according to the rule:

$$\hat{J} = r - \beta$$

Now, however, capital forms only a part of the wealth of the representative capitalist. In fact, $K = J/\theta$ so that:

$$\hat{K} = \hat{J} - \hat{\theta} = r - \beta - \hat{\theta}$$

One of the main channels through which the pricing of land (or the global environment) affects the scale and rate of the accumulation of capital is through the absorption of a part of capitalist saving in the appreciation of land (or emission permit) prices.

Innovation

We model technical change along the same lines as in Chapter 2 as purely input-augmenting, and thus as changes in the effectivity coefficients, x, ρ, and u. Both the Duménil-Lévy and Kennedy models of induced technical change suggest that the proportional rates of increase of these parameters are functions of the shares of the respective input costs, so that, in the case where land is priced, $\hat{x} = \gamma[\omega]$, $\hat{\rho} = \chi[\zeta - \omega]$, and $\hat{u} = \upsilon[1 - \zeta]$. We maintain the assumptions that $\gamma' > 0$, $\chi' > 0$, and $\upsilon' > 0$.

Labor supply and wages

The labor supply, L, grows at the rate n. We write $\overline{L} = xL$ for the effective labor supply, and $\lambda = \overline{L}/u$ for the effective labor supply-effective land ratio.

Writing $\overline{w} = w/x$ for the (output) wage per effective employed worker, and following Goodwin's model of the labor market as in Chapter 2, we suppose that the wage per employed worker rises and falls with the employment ratio, $e = N/L = \overline{N}/\overline{L}$, according to the law $\hat{w} = \delta(e - e_0)$, where δ is a coefficient measuring the responsiveness of the wage to the employment ratio, and $e_0 = 1$ is an exogenously given employment level at which the wage neither rises nor falls, normalized to unity.

The Goodwin–Kennedy model with land

We can describe the model as a dynamical system in the state variables $\overline{w}, z, \rho$, and λ. Logarithmically differentiating $z = \rho K/u$, we get $\hat{z} = \hat{K} + \chi - \upsilon$. Using $\hat{K} = r - \beta - \hat{\theta}$, and $\hat{\theta} = \hat{\theta}_{\overline{w}}\hat{\overline{w}} + \hat{\theta}_z\hat{z}$, where $\hat{\theta}_{\overline{w}} = \theta_{\overline{w}}\overline{w}/\theta$ is the elasticity of θ with respect to $\overline{w}$, and similarly for the other variables, we see that

$$\hat{z} = r - \beta - \hat{\theta}_{\overline{w}}\hat{\overline{w}} - \hat{\theta}_z\hat{z} + \chi - \upsilon$$

so that

$$(1 + \hat{\theta}_z)\hat{z} = r - \beta - \hat{\theta}_{\overline{w}}\hat{\overline{w}} + \chi - \upsilon$$

Similarly $\hat{\lambda} = \gamma + n - \upsilon$. Thus, we can write the model, remembering that $\zeta[z] = g'[z]/\overline{g}[z]$, and $\omega[\overline{w}, z] = \overline{w}/\overline{g}[z]$:

$$\hat{\overline{w}} = \delta\left(\frac{z}{\lambda} - 1\right) - \gamma[\omega] \tag{3.1}$$

$$\hat{z} = \frac{\rho(\zeta\overline{g}[z] - \overline{w}) - \beta - \hat{\theta}_{\overline{w}}\hat{\overline{w}} + \chi[\zeta - \omega] - \upsilon[1 - \zeta]}{1 + \hat{\theta}_z} \tag{3.2}$$

$$\hat{\rho} = \chi(\zeta - \omega) \tag{3.3}$$

$$\hat{\lambda} = \gamma[\omega] + n - \upsilon[1 - \zeta] \tag{3.4}$$

When land is priced, $\zeta = \zeta^P[z]$. When land is not priced, the same equations describe the evolution of the economy, substituting $\zeta = 1$ for the production share.

A steady state in the land-constrained economy with endogenous technical change requires $\chi[\zeta^* - \omega^*] = 0$ and $\gamma[\omega^*] + n = \upsilon[1 - \zeta^*]$. If land is not priced, $\zeta = 1$, which will generally prevent both of these equations from being satisfied, and thus rule out the existence of a steady state. When land is priced, and technical change is sufficiently responsive to the input shares, these two conditions can determine steady-state shares ζ^* and ω^*, and indirectly the steady-state $\gamma^* = \gamma[\omega^*]$ and $\upsilon^* = \upsilon[1 - \zeta^*]$. Since $\zeta' < 0$, z^* is uniquely determined in the priced land case from $\zeta^* = \zeta^P[z^*]$. Then $\overline{w}^* = \omega^* \bar{g}[z^*]$. Thus the steady-state environmental stress, z^*, steady-state wage share ω^*, and the steady-state effective wage $\overline{w}^*$ are determined purely by the mechanism of endogenous technical change. The labor market and accumulation then determine the steady-state effectivity of capital, $\rho^* = (\beta + n + \gamma^*)/(\zeta^* \bar{g}[z^*] - \overline{w}^*)$ and the steady-state effective population-land ratio, $\lambda^* = z^*/(1 + \gamma^*/\delta)$.

The steady-state comparative dynamics of the priced land model still insulate distribution from capitalist thrift, but not from the growth of labor, n, which appears in the $\hat{\lambda} = 0$ expression. Since a rise in n requires a rise in the steady-state rate of land-augmenting technical progress, while the condition $\chi[\zeta^* - \omega^*] = 0$ determines the steady-state profit share, $\zeta^* - \omega^*$, $\zeta_n^* < 0$, and $\omega_n^* < 0$. The steady-state effective population-land ratio, λ^*, is also insulated from capitalist thrift by the adjustment of ρ^*, but rises with n due to the consequent increase in the production-effective land ratio, $z_n^* > 0$ and fall in the rate of growth of labor effectivity, $\gamma_n^* < 0$ (see Foley, 2003, for a complete discussion of the difference in growth paths when the scarce land resource is priced and unpriced).

Some simulated growth paths

Figure 3.1 shows simulated growth paths from this model in both the priced land regime and the unpriced land regime (see also Foley, 2003). The bottom right-hand graph in the figure shows the dramatic difference in the path of land productivity. When land is priced and the mechanism of endogenous technical change is operating, the productivity of land rises steadily and the rate of increase of land productivity converges to the level required to sustain population growth and capital accumulation. As a result

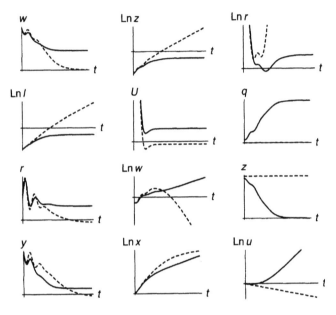

Figure 3.1 Growth paths generated by the model with endogenous technical change
    when land constrains output. The priced land regime is shown in black,
    and the unpriced land regime in gray. The priced land system moves
    toward a steady state after a transient Goodwin predator–prey cycle. The
    unpriced land regime fails to find a steady state, and drives the effective
    wage and wage share toward zero. In this simulation, $\beta = 0.1, n = 0.02$,
    $\delta = 0.05, \rho = 0.5, \gamma = 0.02$, the output function is $g[z] = (z^{(\tau-1)/\tau} +$
    $\eta/(1 - \eta))^{\tau/(\tau-1)}$ with $\eta = 0.5$ and $\tau = 0.5$, and the technical change
    functions are $\gamma[\psi] = -0.015 + 0.05\psi$, $\chi[\zeta - \psi] = -0.04 + 0.1(\zeta - \psi)$,
    and $\upsilon[1 - \zeta] = -0.005 + 0.15(1 - \zeta)$.

the effective population-land ratio, λ, and the environmental stress, z, both
stabilize in a sustainable pattern. When land is not priced, land productivity
drifts downward, leading to an unsustainable steady growth in the effective
population-land ratio and environmental stress. The effective wage in this
simulation is eventually forced down to zero in the unpriced land regime,
while it stabilizes in the priced land regime.

These simulations also underline the importance of the wealth effect in
pricing land. When land is priced capitalist households divert some of their
saving to maintaining their portfolio of land, which reduces the accumulation
of capital and environmental stress.

Closed and open loops

The most important conclusion to be drawn from this analysis is that when land constrains production and is not appropriated, there is no feedback mechanism to influence the bias of technical change to favor land, and hence in general no steady state. When a steady state fails to exist because land is not priced, the long-run growth path of the system shows a gradual shift of income toward the profit share (which is the residual). As the profit share becomes larger, induced technical change is biased toward a labor-using, capital-saving pattern, which further drives down the wage and the wage share, possibly toward zero. The very high profit share induces very high rates of capital accumulation. This process continues until the pressure of production on the global environment drives productivity of the labor-capital input close to zero, the catastrophe foreseen by prophets of environmental doom. The basic problem in this scenario is that there is no closed loop feedback connecting the increase in the marginal productivity of land (or the global environment) to technical changes that will be land- (or environment-) saving and thus reduce the stress of production on the environment. In this open loop situation the capitalist economy runs into the "tragedy of the commons" on the grand scale, the new commons being global environmental quality.

When land is appropriated, on the other hand, a closed loop feedback between the scarcity of environmental resources (or, equivalently, the stress of production on the environment) and environment-saving technical change can establish itself. If the technical change mechanism is sufficiently respon-sive, this feedback can stabilize the economy on a viable and sustainable long-run growth path in which land saving technical change just matches the rate of increase of production, so that the stress of production on the environment is stabilized.

Paths to sustainability

In this model the self-organization of technical change in the capitalist economy through feedback from the productivity of inputs to the pat-tern of technical change provides a path to sustainability of the capital accumulation and growth processes. The key element in establishing this feedback is the conversion of the scarcity value of global environmental quality into real money costs and incomes through an emissions permit scheme. Once the scarcity of the global environment creates a cost signal, the model supposes that the inherent tendency of capitalism to seek out technical change that reduces cost can stabilize the stress of production on the environment.

Implementing emission permits

There are interesting problems of implementation of this path to environmental sustainability. Given the scientific uncertainty that surrounds the global warming problem, should we put a system of controls into place, or would it be wiser to wait until the scientific controversies have been resolved? Is a system of permits superior to a system of emissions fees or taxes, which would also create a real monetary incentive to environment-saving technical change? If a permit scheme is put in place, should the environment be privatized by allowing private households and firms to own emission permits, or appropriated by the global society as a whole through having an international agency or national governments own the permits? Through what mechanism would we decide how many permits to issue? How should the permits be distributed initially among countries and regions?

It seems to me that there is a strong argument that prudence in this case lies on the side of putting an emissions control system into place, even if there is a substantial probability that it will prove unnecessary once scientific research has dispelled some of the uncertainties that surround the issue. If we begin to follow an emissions-control path of the type outlined above, it would not mean declines in consumption or standards of living for current generations. Resources for investments in cleaner technology would come by reducing investment in traditional sectors. If after a few decades of following this policy we discovered that global warming was not actually a significant problem, the costs of the policy would amount to some excess investment in clean power generation and a corresponding underinvestment in traditional sectors, an imbalance that another few decades could easily correct. But if the classical theory of induced technical change is correct, deferring control mechanisms also defers the allocation of research and development efforts on cleaner technologies. If global warming is indeed a threat to future generations' welfare, the sooner that we develop cleaner technologies, the easier will be the process of protecting them.

There are strong technical arguments in favor of a permit scheme rather than emissions fees for the control of greenhouse gases. Weitzman (1974) has shown that the choice between taxes and quantity constraints as methods of controlling an activity that generates an externality depends in large part on whether we are more certain of the marginal social cost imposed by the activity (in this case greenhouse gas emission), or the socially optimal level of the activity. If we know that the activity has a relatively constant marginal social cost over a wide range of activity levels, it is easier to estimate the tax that corresponds to that marginal social cost and to let market forces adjust the level of the activity than to legislate the socially optimal level of the activity. If, on the other hand, social marginal costs change in a highly nonlinear fashion with the level of the activity, as is the case for the global warming scenario, it is easier to set the level and let the market determine the marginal cost through bidding for the rights to emit. In the case of greenhouse gas concentrations in the atmosphere it seems likely that we have a much better idea of the absolute carrying capacity of the atmosphere than we have of the social marginal costs of global warming. This is not to say that we have very good estimates of the greenhouse-gas carrying capacity of the atmosphere, since the geophysical models of global warming are relatively new, primitive, and highly controversial. But our ability to estimate the social marginal cost of global warming at its optimal level is even more limited. Furthermore, the process of induced technical change on which the whole argument of this chapter is based envisions constantly changing social marginal costs of emissions as cleaner technologies emerge. A system of emission taxes would have to be constantly revised to respond to these changes. Given the difficulty the international political system has in negotiating issues that involve major economic interests, it is unlikely that it could respond quickly and accurately enough to keep the tax rate anywhere near an optimal level. With a system of permits, on the other hand, the market is constantly re-valuing the permit royalties through competitive bidding for emissions rights. As cleaner technologies emerge to reduce the stress of production on the environment, the royalties determined by the market will tend to adjust much faster than an administered emissions fee or tax.

The question of whether permits should be owned by private households and firms or by national governments or by an international agency raises fundamental controversies over the values of socialism and capitalism. The very idea of appropriating a social resource like global environmental quality and establishing a market in it is objectionable to some socialists, who see the commodity form itself as the main flaw in capitalist society. On the other hand, it is hard to see any more positive step to socialism on a world scale than the establishment of the principle of social ownership of environmental assets. Given the current highly mixed pattern of government and private ownership in the world economy, it is unlikely that a single pattern of ownership of emission permits could be established over the whole world. Initially, it is very likely that the permits would be allocated to national governments rather than to a single international organization. National governments might then either hold the permits as an asset for their own account, or auction off permit rights to private firms on the model of the auctioning of the radio frequency spectrum.

The two most contentious issues an emission permit scheme will face, I suspect, are the question of the total amount of permits to be issued, or, equivalently, the mechanism through which the total number of permits will be decided, and the problem of deciding the principle on which the initial allocation of permits will be based.

The problem of deciding the total amount of permits to be issued is complicated by the large scientific uncertainties that surround the global warming scenario. Different geophysical models predict quite different paths of average global temperature for the same path of greenhouse gas emissions. Furthermore, the actual economic costs of any degree of global warming are difficult to predict accurately. Thus we can foresee a polarization of opinion over the issue of the amount of permits between those who favor a cautious policy based on an extremely limited issue of permits, because they are concerned that current science may underestimate the costs of global warming, and those who favor a minimal policy of restriction of emissions designed to create a market for the permits and a monetary cost for emissions as an incentive to research into cleaner technologies. Outside these two poles it is easy to foresee extreme groups arguing on the one hand for zero emissions, on the ground that humanity has no right to alter the global climate, and on the other hand for no emission restrictions at all on the grounds that the benefits of economic growth outweigh any possible damage to the environment. (I have argued above that these extreme views are economically fallacious, since if there is indeed an externality involved in greenhouse gas emissions, there must be a Pareto-improving allocational alternative, and it is unlikely to imply zero emissions.)

The question of the initial allocation of emission permits, once a total quantity has been determined, is largely a problem of allocating the substantial revenues that will be generated by the permit system, but is a crucial aspect of the whole scheme. The political conflict inherent in an emissions permit scheme is mitigated, as we have seen, by the presumed existence of a Pareto-improving allocation. It ought to be possible to find a range of initial permit allocations that all, or almost all, nations would view as superior to the option of uncontrolled emissions. But it may not be so easy to find this range, or to settle on a compromise system within it. Two benchmark principles represent the extremes of this distributional conflict. One scheme would allocate permits in proportion to current emissions. This would lead to minimal disruption of current patterns of energy generation, but would give the lion's share of the permits and permit revenues to the developed capitalist countries, and force developing countries to bid permits away, perhaps at high prices, to build new energy and transportation infrastructure. An alternative principle would be to allocate permits in proportion to population. In this case, the developing countries would get the majority of the permits, and the developed countries would have to start paying substantial royalties to them to maintain their existing high-emission energy and transportation technologies. The developing countries ought to be enthusiastic about this benchmark, because it would guarantee large flows of revenue from the developed to the developing world, and constitute a welcome windfall for developing economies. But the developed capitalist economies would by the same token presumably resist this plan, on the ground that it would impose substantial net costs on their economies. But the existence of two broad principles each of which would be acceptable to one of the main participant constituencies indicates that some compromise between the two principles ought to be able to satisfy both groups of countries. In fact, this analysis suggests that a negotiation might center on allocating a certain proportion of the permits on the basis of population and the rest on the basis of historical emissions. Somewhere along the line between 100 percent to population and 100 percent to historic emissions there ought to be a range of options attractive to both the developing and developed economies.

These considerations lead to the conclusion that it would be prudent to initiate a permits scheme with a relatively liberal total emissions cap, at least in the beginning, as soon as possible. The implementation and enforcement of an elaborate and almost unprecedented system of world controls on greenhouse gas emissions will take considerable shaking down, and the incentives to evasion of the system will be smaller if the cap is relatively liberal and the royalty levels moderate, at least in the beginning of the system. If current generations made this effort, they could significantly broaden the options humanity will face in this respect over the next three centuries.

Economic policy and self-organizing complexity

The idea of using an emissions-permit system to mitigate the effects of global warming might appear completely wrong-headed. It might be argued that the whole problem of global environmental deterioration is a side-effect of commodity production and the growing division of labor that the commodity form of production sustains. It seems illogical to respond to the problems of commoditization by extending the commodity form into yet another realm, but that is precisely what the emissions permit system does, by effectively turning the carrying capacity of the global atmosphere into an exchange value.

From the point of view of complex systems theory, however, this type of policy response does not seem so paradoxical. In the complexity perspective the crucial issue is the flow of information within the system that facilitates its adaptability and self-organization. The creation of new markets and new prices is important from this angle because it increases the range of information the system produces and can react to. There might be other policies that could also generate this flow of information (in this case the effective cost of greenhouse gas emissions) but it is doubtful that any of them would interact as well with global capitalist market institutions as an emissions permit market.

There are perhaps deeper lessons to be learned from this case about the construction of economic policy. Direct interventions (such as direct controls or the outlawing of certain kinds of activities) have counter-intuitive effects in complex systems. Because the self-organization of such systems is so robust, they have a way of restoring patterns despite attempts at direct intervention. It may be the subtler and more effective path to alter the conditions under which the system organizes itself by changing its information structure, and thus put the powerful forces of self-organization in the service of the policy-maker rather than opposing them directly.

4 The new economy and the population of the Earth

The size of the human population of the earth and its impact on the quality of human life has been a recurring theme of anxiety and discussion in the last half-century. Much of this discussion is based on two premises: that the size of the earth's population is an important factor in determining the quality of life, because the planet's resources, surface, and environment have a limited capacity to support human life; and that the population will tend to grow uncontrollably without some type of intervention. This type of thinking leads to popular doomsday scenarios in which overpopulation destroys the quality of life. It also supports a kind of population determinism, which sees the absolute size of the world's population as the main determinant of world economic welfare. (Much of this chapter has been published as Foley, 2000b. The idea that increasing returns might stabilize human populations arose during the visit of David Colander to my undergraduate Political Economy class at Barnard College. I am indebted to Adalmir Marquetti for his help in collecting the data.)

These ideas have a close relation to Classical political economy, particularly to the views of Malthus and Ricardo on population and diminishing returns. Their sudden vogue after the Second World War arose because the second half of the twentieth century did indeed see an explosion in world population, coinciding with the extension of European and American capitalist institutions, infrastructure, and medical care to the greater part of the world.

I tend to accept the first premise of this discussion. The size of the human population probably does have a substantial impact on the quality of life. But for the levels of world population we have historically experienced and are likely ever to reach, the larger the population the better the quality of life tends to be. I tend, on the other hand, to doubt the second premise. A correct application of Classical political economy methods to the problem of determining the world equilibrium of population predicts a stabilization of population at a relatively high per-capita income, and far from the diminishing returns at the heart of Malthus' and Ricardo's vision. I suspect that world population will stabilize somewhere around 20–40 percent above its current level of six billion, that is, in the range of seven to eight and a half billion people, with world per capita income about 20–40 percent higher than it was in 1990. This is a large, but manageable, population. The population problems of the twenty-first century are likely to be quite different from those of the last half of the twentieth century. Stable populations have an age structure with a much higher proportion of older, retired, and therefore not economically active people. Furthermore, it is likely that the stabilization of total world population and income will come about through a sharp polarization between countries with rich aging populations which cannot reproduce themselves and countries with poor, younger populations which are growing.

Smith and Malthus

The Classical political economists regarded the problem of population as an aspect of the analysis of capital accumulation and growth. In this view, population growth is a consequence of economic development, and the size of the population is regulated by economic factors.

Malthus based his analysis on two central postulates: that increasing standards of living *raise* net population growth rates by reducing mortality (particularly infant mortality) and raising fertility, and that the standard of living is regulated by *diminishing* returns to human productive activity in the face of limited land, including natural resources. The implication of these two postulates is Malthus' famous, frightening, image of a stable demographic equilibrium at which high mortality balances high fertility at a low absolute average standard of living. Increases in natural resources and labor productivity, in Malthus' framework, raise the equilibrium level of population without much altering its low standard of living. Despite a widespread recognition that this is not really how the modern world economy works, this Malthusian nightmare continues to lurk behind the discussion of population questions.

History has not borne out Malthus' postulates. While the early stages of economic growth did indeed produce population explosions in many countries stemming from a rapid fall in mortality with improved sanitation, nutrition, and public health, there is an equally strong longer-run pattern of falling fertility rates stemming from reduced infant mortality, increased educational and economic opportunities for women, and better public and private financial provision for old age. The spread of cheap and accessible contraception has facilitated this demographic transition to lower mortality and fertility rates. Thus the first of the Malthusian presumptions has not been borne out by the historical record. Economic demographers have argued convincingly that the demographic transition is a reliable consequence of economic development.

Nor have the past 250 years of historically rapid increases in economic production and population exhibited signs of diminishing returns in the face of limited natural resources and land, despite the ominous indications of environmental and ecological degradation that have accumulated over the last fifty years. The explosive increase in the world human population has in fact been accompanied by increases in economic productivity and average standards of living, although these increases have been extremely unequally distributed both between and within countries. The causes of this epochal rise in productivity are less well-agreed-on among social scientists. Economists tend to attribute it to a change in "technology," stemming from an accumulation of scientific and technical knowledge that proceeds either autonomously as the fruit of human curiosity and ingenuity, or endogenously from incentives for cost-reducing technological innovation.

Smith, who identified the division of labor as the underlying condition for technological progress, would perhaps not have been surprised by the unfolding patterns of world population and production. For Smith a larger population would imply opportunities for a much wider and deeper division of labor, both at the detailed level in particular production processes, and at the social level through regional specialization and trade. Smith's vision implies, contrary to the postulate of diminishing returns, that a larger population, up to some limit, will have higher rather than lower productivity. If this relationship holds, it has important consequences for the stability of the world population. Curiously, the economic increasing returns posited by Smith due to the division of labor is precisely the condition necessary to stabilize human populations that are undergoing the demographic transition to lower fertility rates. These considerations suggest that the current world population may be quite close to an equilibrium stabilized by falling fertility rather than rising mortality. Autonomous technical progress will have the consequence of lowering, rather than raising, this Smithian equilibrium world population.

Stable and unstable demographic equilibria

It is convenient to consider population dynamics in terms of "total female fertility," the average number of children born over the fertile phase of a woman's life cycle. Assuming a sex ratio in births close to 50 percent, population will stabilize in the long-run when total female fertility is 2. This measure focuses on average rates of reproduction, avoiding the complications of mortality rates among men and women past childbearing age. By the same token, an analysis based on total female fertility will abstract from the age composition of the population and its transitional dynamics, issues which are of central policy and social importance.

Malthus' postulates of falling mortality, especially infant mortality, and rising fertility with a rising standard of living, imply that total female fertility will rise with the standard of living. We will identify standard of living with household income, and assume that household income is proportional to per-capita economic output, $x = X/L$, where X is Gross Domestic Product (corrected for inflation), and L is population. Measuring total fertility, f, on the horizontal axis and per-capita output, x, on the vertical axis, Malthus' assumptions apply to the positive segment of the income-fertility relation sketched in Figure 4.1.

In this figure, a Malthusian demographic equilibrium, x_M, occurs at the per-capita output corresponding to a fertility rate of 2 on the upward sloping segment of the income-fertility relation. This equilibrium will be stable if a rising population lowers per-capita output, x. Malthus and Ricardo took this as axiomatic, relying on the presumption of economic diminishing returns to increases in labor (and capital) in the face of limited land. Thus, Malthus' theory implicitly assumes that the economy lies on the downward sloping segment of the population-per-capita output relation sketched in Figure 4.2.

Malthus' postulate on the relation between income and fertility was incorrect, or at least incomplete. Fertility eventually falls with rising incomes, so that there are two potential demographic equilibria, as Figure 4.1 illustrates, the low per-capita output Malthusian equilibrium and another high per-capita output equilibrium, the Smithian equilibrium, x_S.

The Smithian equilibrium will be stable if an increase in the population *raises* productivity and incomes. If incomes rise above the Smithian

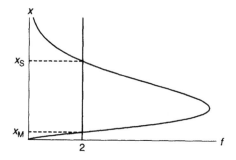

Figure 4.1 The theoretical income-fertility relation has both an upward sloping segment, corresponding to Malthus' assumption of rising fertility with income, and a downward sloping segment, corresponding to the demographic transition in which fertility falls with income. There are two equilibrium levels of per-capita output, at which total fertility equals 2, the Malthusian equilibrium x_M, and the Smithian equilibrium, x_S.

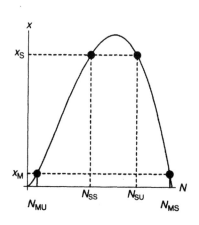

Figure 4.2 When the population-per-capita output relation has both a rising portion, representing the effects of the division of labor, and a falling portion, representing the effects of diminishing returns, there are potentially two Malthusian and two Smithian equilibria. The low-population Malthusian equilibrium and the high-population Smithian equilibrium are unstable, while the low-population Smithian equilibrium and the high population Malthusian equilibrium are stable.

equilibrium, fertility will fall below its replacement level and the population will start to decline. If incomes are an increasing function of population size, as Smith argued in his discussion of the division of labor, incomes will decline with the fall in population, and fertility will increase, tending to restore the equilibrium.

The stability of Smithian demographic equilibrium requires that the economy lie on a rising portion of the population-per-capita output relation. Smith's theory of the division of labor suggests that this curve has a rising portion, in which the division of labor effect is dominant, and then perhaps a falling portion in which diminishing returns due to land limitations take over, as in Figure 4.2.

If the effects of the division of labor are sufficiently strong that per-capita output can reach the levels required for the Smithian demographic equilibrium, there are actually four equilibrium levels of population, two Malthusian, and two Smithian. The Smithian equilibrium on the rising part of the population-per-capita output curve and the Malthusian equilibrium on the falling part are stable, while the other two are unstable. (There is another stable equilibrium at the origin.) The two unstable equilibria mark the boundary between the basins of attraction of the stable equilibria.

The stable Smithian demographic equilibrium occurs at a relatively high average per-capita output, and is stabilized by the fall in fertility occasioned by increases in per-capita output and hence household income. It has features which are counter-intuitive from the point of view of diminishing returns. An autonomous *rise* of the population-per-capita output relation at the stable Smithian equilibrium would lead to a *lower* equilibrium population, with an unchanged level of equilibrium output per capita. An autonomous fall in the income-fertility relationship at the stable Smithian equilibrium would lead to a lower equilibrium level of per-capita output and, for a given population-per-capita output relation, a lower population.

In order for the economy to fall into the Malthusian–Ricardian equilibrium of generalized misery, the population would have to overshoot not just the stable Smithian equilibrium, but also the unstable Smithian equilibrium, entering the realm of strongly diminishing returns, at a low enough level of per-capita output that fertility is above replacement level.

This line of argument suggests that the classical methods of analysis employed by Ricardo and Malthus are capable of yielding important insights into the long-run dynamics of world population. Malthus erred not in seeking a stable demographic equilibrium, but in failing to consider the possibilities of increasing returns and declining fertility with standard of living as an alternative stabilizing feedback relationship on population.

Evidence

It is possible to calibrate these ideas roughly with empirical data. Maddison (1995) has made careful estimates of world output from 1820 to 1992, together with estimates of world population. Economic output is measured in Gross World Product corrected for inflation to 1990 Geary-Khamis dollars $\$_{1990}$, a standard measure of purchasing-power. The estimation of output over very long periods of time requires the comparison of prices for disparate bundles of commodities, and involves a large number of methodological assumptions, so that the results should be used cautiously. Figure 4.3 plots per-capita output against world population over this period. X is Gross World Product, N is world population, and $x = X/N$ is world per-capita output.

If we interpret this plot as the population-per-capita output relation, it strongly confirms Smith's assumption of increasing per-capita output with increasing world population, and suggests that each one billion increase in world population corresponds to an increase in per-capita output of about $\$_{1990}1,000$. Other interpretations of this data, however, are possible.

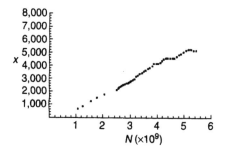

Figure 4.3 Angus Maddison's data on world population and economic output strongly suggest that the world economy is on the upward sloping branch of the population-per-capita output relation. It is possible to fit these data points very well with a linear equation, which suggests that each one billion increase in world population raises per-capita output by about $\$_{1990}1,000$.

For example, the real population-per-capita output relation might be much flatter, or even downward sloping, at each time period, but shifting upward autonomously over time.

Summers and Heston (1991) have compiled an extensive data set, the Penn World Tables, measuring output for many countries in the period 1960–1992, Adalmir Marquetti has combined this with data on national populations and fertility, to create a data set, the Extended Penn World Tables, from which the income-fertility relation can be estimated. (These tables can be downloaded from http://homepage.newschool.edu/~foleyd/epwt, or http://pessoal.portoweb.com.br/aam.) The Penn World Tables measures output in 1985 constant purchasing power dollars, which appear to be the equivalent of about $\$_{1990}1.20$. In these figures the EPWT output measures have been multiplied by 1.2 to put the two data series on a roughly comparable basis.

Total female fertility rates by country for the years 1970 and 1990 are plotted against per capita output in Figures 4.4 and 4.5, which also show nonlinear weighted and unweighted fits to the data for each year. These lines are fitted using the Robust Loess method (Cleveland, 1993), with each data point weighted by the country's population in the weighted fits. A rapid decline in fertility at most levels of per-capita output is apparent.

Two factors are at work in lowering world fertility. First, there is a movement along the income-fertility schedule as incomes rise. But it is clear even from this rather crude evidence that there is a substantial downward shift over time of the income-fertility schedule itself. In other words, fertility is falling over time even at constant levels of income.

Estimation of the world stable Smithian equilibrium population and per-capita output is complicated by the extremely uneven world distribution of income across countries, and the rapid shift in the income-fertility relation indicated by Figures 4.4 and 4.5.

In an effort to separate the pure Smith effect (the decline in fertility due to rising income along a given income-fertility relation) from shifts in the income-fertility relation over time, we can calculate projected world fertility from the weighted non-linear fit estimating the income-fertility relation for a given year with the actual per-capita outputs of countries in other years. Table 4.1 reports the results of this calculation, using the income-fertility relations estimated for 1990, and for the whole data set ("all") to project fertility for other years.

These calculations suggest that the pure Smith effect is a fall of 0.6–0.9 in fertility for a rise of $\$_{1990}1,000$ in world per-capita output.

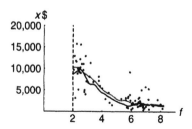

Figure 4.4 Each data point represents total female fertility and per-capita output for a particular country over a five-year average period, centered on 1970, with Weighted Robust Loess fits (black), and unweighted Loess fits (gray). The demographic transition, in which fertility falls with income, is strongly marked.

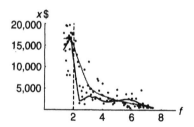

Figure 4.5 Each data point represents total female fertility and per-capita output for a particular country over a five-year average period, centered on 1990, with Weighted Robust Loess fits (black), and unweighted Loess fits (gray). The demographic transition, in which fertility falls with income, is strongly marked. The non-linear fit for 1990 suggests that the Smithian demographic equilibrium would occur at an income level of about $_{1990}11,000$.

Since 1990 world fertility was about 3.4, 1.4 above the replacement level of 2, these very rough estimates suggest that Smithian equilibrium would be reached with an increase in per-capita world output of $_{1990}1,500$–$2,500$, corresponding to an increase in world population of 1.5–2.5 billion above its 1990 levels. Thus from these considerations we might expect world population to stabilize at a level of 7.5–8.5 billion at a per-capita output of $_{1990}6,500$–$7,500$, even without any further shift in the income-fertility relation.

Table 4.1 World levels of fertility are projected by apply-
ing fitted income-fertility relations for 1990
and the whole data set ("All") to actual levels of country income in selected years, and
compared with actual world fertility and per-
capita output. The 1990 projection shows a
drop of 0.9 in fertility per $1990 1,000, and the
whole data set projection shows a drop of 0.6
in fertility per $1990 1,000

Year	1990 *proj f*	All *proj f*	Actual *f*	x
1975	4.91	4.49	4.7	3,870
1980	4.48	4.2	4.08	4,310
1985	4.06	3.94	3.74	4,500
1990	3.8	3.77	3.37	5,050

If the autonomous fall in fertility we observe in the income-fertility relations continues, the stable Smithian equilibrium would occur at even lower
levels of world population and per-capita income. In fact, there appears to be
a real chance that the world population might overshoot its equilibrium level,
leading to a period of secular decline in world population. Such a development would bring problems of its own with it, including a chronic tendency
toward an age-distribution of population unbalanced toward the old.

Population, innovation, and sustainability

These considerations suggest that it will, in fact, not be very difficult to
achieve a stable world population only modestly larger than our current
numbers, which should make the problems of managing population-related
environmental and resource problems more tractable.

The longer-term picture of world population depends critically on the
degree to which innovation and technical change are purely the effect of the
increasing division of labor, as Smith suggested, or have an autonomous
component rooted in the advance of knowledge which will continue to raise
the population-per-capita income relationship over time.

If the division of labor is the predominant factor shaping innovation and
productivity increase, then stabilizing world population will also stabilize
productivity. This is a scenario of the "maturing" or "stagnation" of the world
capitalist economy. Instead of the constant flow of productivity-enhancing
innovations we have become accustomed to over the last two centuries.

human society after fifty or a hundred years would have to adapt to a relatively unchanging technology. Given the important role increasing productivity and increasing standards of living have played in stabilizing the social relations of capitalist society, one wonders whether such a maturation of the world capitalist society would not be accompanied by greatly increased conflict over the distribution of income and power.

If, on the other hand, autonomous labor productivity-enhancing technical change will continue even with a stable world population, it will tend, as we have seen, to lower the equilibrium level of population at a constant level of income. How would this come about? As labor productivity increased, fertility rates would tend to fall below replacement, leading to a decline in world population. This decline in world population would, according to the Smith effect, reduce labor productivity, offsetting the autonomous increase from the innovation process. World per-capita income would tend to remain stable at the level consistent with replacement fertility, while world population would drift downward. This scenario is easier on the environment and world resources, but raises the same spectre of increased conflict over distribution as a result of stabilized average standards of living.

In either of these scenarios one can imagine a revival of "class" politics, arising not from the "absolute" immiserization that Marx initially predicted for capitalist society, but from "relative" immiserization. Workers with stagnant standards of living much lower than those of wealthy capitalists might reasonably question the social utility of the existing system of property relations.

Distribution

Even if the emergence of a stable Smithian equilibrium in world population solves some of the problems of sustainability that increasingly preoccupy us, it will not directly address the distribution of income levels among countries. It is likely that the Smithian equilibrium will be attained with a very unequal distribution of world output and income. A large minority of the world population will live in very productive, high-income countries with low fertility and aging populations, offset by a majority living in relatively unproductive, low-income countries with higher fertility and younger populations. World population may indeed stabilize, but only with increasing imbalances in income and numbers between regions.

What effects will these imbalances have? Broadly speaking these fall into two categories, productive and reproductive arbitrage opportunities and pressures.

Productive arbitrage opportunities will arise because the rich countries will have chronic shortages of labor and surpluses of capital, while poor countries will have chronic shortages of capital and surpluses of labor. Arbitrage suggests either the movement of capital to the poor countries through foreign investment, or the movement of labor to the rich countries through migration. (This emerging world pattern is in contrast to the earlier globalization of the nineteenth century, which was driven by imbalances between capital-labor and land among regions of the world.) The initial phases of these two processes constitute the patterns that we now call "globalization." The pressures underlying movements of capital and labor between rich and poor countries will, if anything, become more pronounced with the gradual stabilization of the world population.

Reproductive arbitrage opportunities will arise because of the tendency for poor countries to specialize in producing children, as the rich countries specialize in producing wealth. Thus, we can expect an explosive growth in the trade in reproduction and its associated services like surrogate parenthood, adoption, and the provision of child-care services between older, richer countries and younger, poorer countries. We have also begun to see the early stages of this phenomenon already.

Existing world institutions are probably inadequate to cope with a huge growth in foreign investment, migration, and trade in reproductive services. We can expect these areas, no less than global environmental problems, to be active areas of policy discussion and institutional innovation in the coming decades.

Challenges and pitfalls

The interaction of systematically falling fertility with rising income and rising per-capita output with rising world population can have a powerful and pervasive long-run impact on world demographic dynamics. Some cautions are in order, however.

In the short-run shifts in the income-fertility and population-per-capita income relations may obscure the underlying equilibrating forces. In fact, if these schedules are not very stable, the whole concept of a stable demographic equilibrium may not have very much explanatory power.

The economic statistics we have are highly imperfect and allow only a very rough estimate of the actual location of the theoretical equilibrium. As we have seen, some of the available data suggest that the world may already be fairly close to the stable Smithian equilibrium, and that an increase in world population of 25–30 percent may be sufficient to bring this equilibrium about. My guess is that the income-fertility relation is relatively well-identified in this data. Since there is evidence that the income-fertility relation is shifting downward, these estimates probably overestimate equilibrium population and equilibrium world per-capita output on this account.

How much can we count on the demographic transition to continue to describe world fertility patterns? The forces tending to lower fertility with increasing income are at root the secularizing forces of capitalist economic development, which creates pervasive pressures for higher educational standards and broader economic opportunities for women, and raises the cost of child-rearing. These broad trends are very deeply-seated in the path of capitalist economic development, but might be disrupted by social developments of a different kind. For example, the rapid growth of fundamentalist religious beliefs in the world's major religions is often accompanied by a denial of women's rights to education and full economic participation, and an explicit attempt to resurrect traditional fertility patterns.

The location and dynamics of the population-per-capita output relation may be much more problematic than I have suggested. Limited data suggest a stable linear correlation between world population and world per-capita income over the last two hundred years. But there are many conceptual and practical problems in the measurement of this relationship. Even if the figures we have used are broadly correct, the interpretation of this correlation is not straightforward. The same correlation could arise if in each period the population-per-capita income relation were in fact downward sloping (consistent with a Malthusian equilibrium), but the relation itself were shifting upward steadily over time due to autonomous technological change and innovation. More detailed and disaggregated studies are necessary to sort out the exact level at which Smith's division of labor effect could be expected to operate, and the impact it might be expected to have at the level of the world economy as a whole. In the past we might have expected the division of labor effect to operate primarily at a regional or national level. If this were true, then the correlation we observe at the world level would arise because world population is acting as an index for the density of regional and national populations. On the other hand, with the increasing global integration of world production, it seems more likely that in the future the division of labor effect will operate at the level of the world economy.

Nonetheless, the scenario of stabilization of world population the Classical method produces with the introduction of the demographic transition and Smithian division of labor integrates and explains many features of contemporary world society. It should surely not be ignored as a likely path, and perhaps should serve as a benchmark against which alternative projections and hypotheses should be tested.

Methods and conclusions

The example of world population underlines again the power of the methods of the Classical political economists. The flaw in Ricardo's and Malthus' arguments as to the long-run tendencies of population lay not in their method of looking for a stable equilibrium of social forces (or, in the language of complex systems theory, for robust self-organizing tendencies of the system), but in the particular shape they believed these forces took. Their strong adherence to a prior belief in a positive relation between fertility and standard of living, and more particularly, in diminishing returns, made what I have here called the Smithian equilibrium of population and output invisible to them. This is perhaps surprising in that both Malthus and Ricardo knew Adam Smith's work well, and we can find in Smith clear hints (which is as much as we can hope for from Smith) of the demographic transition (Smith, 1937, ch. VIII). The impact of growing population on labor productivity is an even more prominent and unambiguous feature of Smith's argument (Smith, 1937, ch. I).

There is a rich vein of insights still waiting to be mined by the methods of the Classical political economists, a vein considerably enriched by the immense profusion of data contemporary economists have to work with. The theory of complex systems provides the larger framework within which these methods can be employed, and which explains their stunning effectiveness.

5 Concluding observations

What are the advantages of regarding capitalist economies as complex, adaptive, self-organizing systems typically far from equilibrium?

First, we can dispense with many of the nagging problems that arise in the representation of firms and households in an equilibrium setting. The vision of market equilibrium requires each firm and household to be in equilibrium as a precondition of the economy to be in equilibrium. This further requires tremendous and unrealistic informational and planning capacities on the part of the firms and households. Firms and households facing risky investment opportunities have to have accurate information about prices of assets at future dates and in detailed contingencies in order to value investment plans. It has always seemed improbable that firms and households in real economies have these information-gathering and processing capacities, and a great part of the theoretical effort generated by the equilibrium research program is directed to weakening or rationalizing these requirements. Because self-organization in complex systems is robust, it requires much less structure in the behavior of firms and households to sustain it, and is compatible with a much wider range of firm and household sophistication. The innovating firms in the endogenous technical change world of Chapters 2 and 3, for example, do not have to evaluate the whole complex path of price changes their innovations set in motion, or even do much more than grope tentatively toward cost reduction.

This freedom is reflected in the much more open modeling methodology suggested by the complex systems approach. The behavior of the agents composing an economy can be both simpler and more closely adapted to particular institutional or historical situations. The researcher's insights or guesses as to behavior that may be critical to the evolution of the economy have wider scope in the complex systems approach.

Second, the complex systems program allows us to acknowledge a much wider range of phenomena in the study of the capitalist economy, and to situate each in a more appropriate and relevant context. For example, the various conceptions of market equilibrium, including both Classical or Neoclassical theories, assume that technology remains constant on the time-scale on which equilibrium or natural prices are formed. But we also know that innovation is central to the competitive process of capitalist economies, and that it leads to a non-stationary evolution of technology. The complex systems approach embraces this duality without embarrassment. There is nothing surprising in a complex system having highly organized, even quasi-equilibrium subsystems. The inherent character of complex systems is to articulate a large number of subsystems which may each be organized in quite different ways.

Third, the complex systems approach should lay to rest the dubious project of detailed forecasting of the economic future. Complex systems are computationally irreducible, or incompressible, in the sense that there is no way of encoding the evolutionary path of the system in a model less complex than the system itself. This feature of real capitalist economies presumably lies behind what appear to be a constant stream of methodological problems that confront the equilibrium research program, for example, the failure of statistical methods in the face of non-stationarity. As I have tried to argue in this book, the study of self-organization can to some degree provide a substitute for detailed forecasting, in that self-organization is responsible for the reproduction of certain key features in economic data. But the study of self-organization inherently avoids the fallacy of thinking that a model of the economy can represent its evolution in detail. Another way to put this point is that the complex systems vision restores the genuine openness of the economic future as an evolutionary process, without requiring the assumption of a definite future equilibrium path (or collection of equilibrium paths) to organize the current behavior of agents as the equilibrium program does. This may seem to be as much a disadvantage as an advantage methodologically, but if the future is genuinely open, it is better to work within a framework that acknowledges that reality.

Classical political economy reflects the combination of a breathtaking openness of vision and a formidable realism concerning human societies. The Classical political economists were fertile speculators concerning the most abstract and general features of economic life, and at the same time

insisted on following out to sometimes unpalatable conclusions the con-
flictual logic of capitalist social relations. We inherit from this period of
intellectual creativity a powerful range of insights into class, distribution,
population, and the dilemmas inherent in the long-run pursuit of capital accumulation. The neoclassical shift of emphasis to the very short-run properties
of market equilibrium, and to a thermodynamic conception of equilibrium
already represents a drastic curtailment of the Classical political economists'
program. The introduction of rigorous mathematical and statistical methods
into the research program of economics in the twentieth century further cir-
cumscribed and narrowed the range of its discourse. Acknowledging the
complexity of the economic system can perhaps restore to us the wide-
ranging unflinchingly realistic speculative freedom the Classical political
economists enjoyed.

Bibliography

Albin, Peter S. and Foley, Duncan K. *Barriers and Bounds to Rationality: Essays on Economic Complexity and Dynamics in Interactive Systems*. Princeton University Press, Princeton, 1998.

Arthur, Brian W. Inductive reasoning and bounded rationality. *American Economic Review*, 84(2): 406–11, 1994.

Burmeister, Edwin. The capital theory controversy. In Heinz D. Kurz (ed.), *Critical Essays on Piero Sraffa's Legacy in Economics*, pp. 305–14. Cambridge University Press, Cambridge, UK, 2000.

Carraro, Carlo (ed.). *Efficiency and Equity of Climate Change Policy*. Kluwer Academic Publishers, Boston, MA, 2000.

Casti, John L. *Reality Rules: II*. Wiley, New York, 1992.

Chichilnisky, Graciela and Heal, Geoffrey M. (eds). *Environmental Markets: Equity and Efficiency*. Columbia University Press, New York, 2000.

Cleveland, William S. *Visualizing Data*. AT&T Bell Laboratories, Hobart Press, Summit, NJ, 1993.

Cline, William R. *The Economics of Global Warming*. Institute for International Economics, Washington, DC, 1997.

Cowan, George A., Pines, David, and Meltzer, David (eds). *Complexity: Metaphors, Models, and Reality*. Addison-Wesley, Reading, MA, 1994.

Drandakis, Emanuel M. and Phelps, Edmund S. A model of induced invention, growth and distribution. *Economic Journal*, 79: 823–40, 1966.

Duménil, Gérard and Lévy, Dominique. *The Economics of the Profit Rate*. Edward Elgar Publishing Company, Aldershot, 1994.

Duménil, Gérard and Lévy, Dominique. A stochastic model of technical change: An application to the U.S. economy. *Metroeconomica*, 46: 213–45, 1995.

Foley, Duncan K. *Understanding Capital: Marx's Economic Theory*. Harvard University Press, Cambridge, MA, Japanese translation, 1988; Italian translation 1994 edition, 1986.

Foley, Duncan K. A statistical equilibrium theory of markets. *Journal of Economic Theory*, 62(2): 321–45, 1994.

Foley, Duncan K. Recent developments in the labor theory of value. *Review of Radical Political Economy*, 32(1): 1–39, 2000a.

Foley, Duncan K. Stabilization of human population through economic increasing returns. *Economic Letters*, 68(3): 309–17, 2000b.

Foley, Duncan K. Endogenous technical change with externalities in a Classical growth model. *Journal of Economic Behavior and Organization* 2003 (forthcoming).

Foley, Duncan K. and Michl, Thomas R. *Growth and Distribution*. Harvard University Press, Cambridge, MA, 1999.

Goodwin, Richard M. A growth cycle. In C. H. Feinstein (ed.), *Socialism, Capitalism and Growth*. Cambridge University Press, Cambridge UK, 1967.

Harcourt, Geoffrey C. *Some Cambridge Controversies in the Theory of Capital*. Cambridge University Press, Cambridge UK, 1972.

Hicks, John R. *Theory of Wages*. Macmillan, London, 1932.

Working Group II Intergovernmental Panel on Climate Change. *Climate Change 2001: Impacts, Adaptation, and Vulnerability: Contribution of Working Group II to the Third Assessment Report of the Intergovernmental Panel on Climate Change*. Cambridge University Press, Cambridge, UK; New York, 2001.

Kauffman, Stuart. *At Home in the Universe*. Penguin, London and New York, 1995.

Kennedy, Charles. Induced bias in innovation and the theory of distribution. *The Economic Journal*, 74(295): 541–7, 1964.

Keynes, John Maynard. *The General Theory of Employment, Interest, and Money*. Macmillan, London, 1936.

Kurz, Heinz D. (ed.). *Critical Essays on Piero Sraffa's Legacy in Economics*. Cambridge University Press, Cambridge, UK, 2000.

Kurz, Heinz D. and Salvadori, Neri. *Theory of Production: A Long-Period Analysis*. Cambridge University Press, Cambridge, UK, 1995.

Maddison, Angus. *Monitoring the World Economy 1820–1992*. OECD Development Center, Paris, 1995.

Malthus, Thomas Robert. *An Essay on Principle of Population*. Penguin, New York, 1985 [1799].

Marx, Karl. *Capital*, Vol. 1. Penguin Books, London and New York, 1976 [1867].

Marx, Karl. *Capital*, Vol. 3. Penguin Books, London and New York, 1981 [1894].

Marx, Karl. *Mathematical Manuscripts of Karl Marx*. New Park Publications, London, 1983.

Mirowski, Philip. *More Heat than Light*. Cambridge University Press, Cambridge, UK, 1992.

Mirowski, Philip. *Machine Dreams: Economics Becomes a Cyborg Science*. Cambridge University Press, Cambridge, UK, 2001.

Okishio, Nobuo. Technical changes and the rate of profit. *Kobe University Economic Review*, 7: 86–99, 1961.

Porter, Theodore M. *The Rise of Statistical Thinking, 1820–1900*. Princeton University Press, Princeton, NJ, 1986.

Ricardo, David. *On the Principles of Political Economy and Taxation*. Cambridge University Press, Cambridge, UK, 1951 [1817].

Salter, W. E. G. *Productivity and Technical Change*. Cambridge University Press, Cambridge, UK, 1960.

Samuelson, Paul A. A theory of induced innovation along Kennedy–Weizsäcker lines. *The Review of Economics and Statistics*, 47(4): 343–56, 1965.

Shah, Anup and Desai, Meghnad. Growth cycles with induced technical change. *The Economic Journal*, 91(364): 1006–10, 1981.

Simon, Herbert A. *Economics, Bounded Rationality and the Cognitive Revolution*. E. Edgar, Brookfield, VT, 1992.

Smith, Adam. *An Inquiry into the Nature and Causes of the Wealth of Nations*. Random House, New York, 1937 [1776].

Solow, Robert M. A skeptical note on the constancy of relative shares. *American Economic Review*, 48(4): 618–31, 1958.

Stigler, Stephen M. *The History of Statistics: The Measurement of Uncertainty before 1900*. Harvard University Press, Cambridge, MA, 1986.

Summers, Robert and Heston, Allen. The Penn World Table (Mark 5): An expanded set of international comparisons, 1950–1988. *Quarterly Journal of Economics*, 106: 327–68, 1991.

van der Ploeg, F. Growth cycles, induced technical change, and perpetual conflict over the distribution of income. *Journal of Macroeconomics*, 9(1): 1–12, 1987.

Weitzman, Martin L. Prices vs. quantities. *Review of Economic Studies*, 41(4): 477–91, 1974.

Wolfram, Steven. *A New Kind of Science*. Wolfram Research, Champaign, IL, 2002.

Young, Allyn Abbott. *Economic Problems, New and Old*. Houghton Mifflin Company, Boston, MA, 1927.

Index